PRESENTED TO:

_____

BY:

_____

Dedicated to my Lord,
who died for me so that I might live.

Published in Nashville, Tennessee, by Thomas Nelson. Thomas Nelson is a registered trademark of Thomas Nelson, Inc.

Published in association with Kristina Holmes at Ebeling & Associates Literary Agency.

Cover design by Studio Gearbox.
Page design by Mandi Cofer.

Thomas Nelson, Inc., titles may be purchased in bulk for educational, business, fund-raising, or sales promotional use. For information, please e-mail SpecialMarkets@ThomasNelson.com.

ISBN 978-1-4041-9003-0

Printed in China

11 12 13 14 15 RRD 6 5 4 3 2 1

Lead
SERVE
Love

BY GREGORY E. LANG

THOMAS NELSON
Since 1798

NASHVILLE   DALLAS   MEXICO CITY   RIO DE JANEIRO

INTRODUCTION

My favorite Bible verse is 1 John 2:6, which says that whoever claims to live in God must walk as Jesus did. Walking with Jesus means putting into action what he has commissioned us to do—to make the gospel known by demonstrating the love of God through our words, deeds, and motives. Jesus charges us to take up his mission in our generation so that his kingdom may continue to come through the work of his people, including you.

Just as Jesus walked from city to city showing mercy and grace to all, we are to be similarly intentional about showing mercy and grace. We should do this as every opportunity arises, even if in unlikely places—when standing next to someone on a street corner, while in line at a grocery store, in the breakroom at work, during rush-hour traffic jams, and in even more far-reaching places and occasions.

This book was written for those who want to walk in the Spirit, to do what Jesus would do, but who need a simple, loving nudge to take those life-changing steps of gospel living. In the following pages you will find one hundred brief, three-word sentences (a friend of mine calls it the "three-ology" theology), each followed by an expository paragraph and a few Bible verses that encourage the behaviors and traits recommended by the three-word sentences. You may begin and end your study of Jesus with this book alone, or, and I hope you will, you may go to your Bible and read the verses I've cited in their full context. The latter process will take more time but leave you more blessed with greater knowledge of the teachings of Jesus, our Lord and Savior.

Turn the page and begin your walk with Jesus today. Along the way, may you lead others to Christ through your faithful, righteous example; may you serve all with a humble, true, and compassionate heart; and may God's love shine through in everything you do.

My Prayer

Father, let me hear the Word clearly that I might understand it. Let not my understanding be dulled by my sinful nature, and soften my heart that I might act faithfully in accordance with what I have heard.

In Jesus' name,
Amen.

1

SMILE AT EVERYONE.

A smile is an easy yet powerful way to show Christ at work in you. Christian living is more than adhering to moral standards of conduct; it is also the demonstration of several graces, including love, joy, and peace. A smile is a one-second chance to extend God's grace and love to someone who otherwise might never see Him. So when you get dressed for the day, put on your smile. Reach into someone's day and make it better. Smile at everyone.

Greet each other with a holy kiss.

2 Corinthians 13:12

. . .

But the Spirit produces the fruit of love, joy, peace, patience, kindness, goodness, faithfulness, gentleness, self-control. There is no law that says these things are wrong.

Galatians 5:22–23

. . .

Do not be bitter or angry or mad. Never shout angrily or say things to hurt others. Never do anything evil. Be kind and loving to each other, and forgive each other just as God forgave you in Christ.

Ephesians 4:31–32

. . .

Be full of joy in the Lord always. I will say again, be full of joy.

Philippians 4:4

. . .

Therefore, as God's chosen people, holy and dearly loved, clothe yourselves with compassion, kindness, humility, gentleness and patience.

Colossians 3:12 NIV

2

Strike up conversations.

You'd be surprised how many people are lonely and think no one cares. So show that *you* care. All it takes is a simple "Hello!" or "How's your day?" It doesn't have to be deep or profound, only sincere. A few spoken words and a few moments of attention can have a powerful effect on someone's day. Extend the comfort that God has given you, and you will surely confound the work of his adversaries. Strike up conversations.

He comforts us every time we have trouble, so when others have trouble, we can comfort them with the same comfort God gives us.

2 Corinthians 1:4

. . .

God has chosen you and made you his holy people. He loves you. So you should clothe yourselves with mercy, kindness, humility, gentleness, and patience.

Colossians 3:12

. . .

Do not forget to entertain strangers, for by so doing some people have entertained angels without knowing it.

Hebrews 13:2 niv

. . .

Open your homes to each other, without complaining.

1 Peter 4:9

. . .

My dear friend, it is good that you help the brothers and sisters, even those you do not know.

3 John 5

3

SAY SOMETHING NICE.

Certainly you enjoy compliments and sincere pleasantries. So does everyone else. As your lips smile, reveal your heart with your kind words. Be cheerful, courteous, and graceful in your speech, attracting others to you so that you might make a new friend. Say something nice.

When you talk, do not say harmful things, but say what people need—words that will help others become stronger. Then what you say will do good to those who listen to you.

EPHESIANS 4:29

. . .

Speak to each other with psalms, hymns, and spiritual songs, singing and making music in your hearts to the Lord.

EPHESIANS 5:19

. . .

When you talk, you should always be kind and pleasant so you will be able to answer everyone in the way you should.

COLOSSIANS 4:6

. . .

Finally, all of you should be in agreement, understanding each other, loving each other as family, being kind and humble. Do not do wrong to repay a wrong, and do not insult to repay an insult. But repay with a blessing, because you yourselves were called to do this so that you might receive a blessing.

1 PETER 3:8–9

4

Share with others.

Share more than just your things, but also your heart, counsel, and time. When you do, you'll enjoy everything more, and so will everyone else. The resources God has entrusted to you should be used in a manner that pleases him. Share them with those having fewer resources but greater needs. Your free and cheerful giving of God's gifts will indeed lead to your blessing. Share with others.

All the believers were together and shared everything. They would sell their land and the things they owned and then divide the money and give it to anyone who needed it. The believers met together in the Temple every day. They ate together in their homes, happy to share their food with joyful hearts.

Acts 2:44–46

. . .

The group of believers were united in their hearts and spirit. All those in the group acted as though their private property belonged to everyone in the group. In fact, they shared everything.

Acts 4:32

. . .

You are rich in everything—in faith, in speaking, in knowledge, in truly wanting to help, and in the love you learned from us. In the same way, be strong also in the grace of giving.

2 Corinthians 8:7

5

MAKE MANY FRIENDS.

To be a friend is to have a friend. You can never have enough friends, but you can have too few. Be zealous, enthusiastic, and accepting, making the needs of your friends your own and helping them, caring for one another in the same loving fellowship as Christ cares for you. You see, it is far easier to introduce a friend to the Lord than an enemy. Make many friends.

Your love must be real. Hate what is evil, and hold on to what is good. Love each other like brothers and sisters. Give each other more honor than you want for yourselves.

Romans 12:9–10

. . .

Christ accepted you, so you should accept each other, which will bring glory to God.

Romans 15:7

. . .

Keep on loving each other as brothers and sisters.

Hebrews 13:1

. . .

So if we say we have fellowship with God, but we continue living in darkness, we are liars and do not follow the truth. But if we live in the light, as God is in the light, we can share fellowship with each other. Then the blood of Jesus, God's Son, cleanses us from every sin.

1 John 1:6–7

6

Encourage your friends.

No friend is more welcomed than the one who encourages you. Make yourself welcomed. Encourage your friends, and stir them to do good deeds so that the cause of Christ may be made stronger in number. Turn them away from false hope and worldly promises, and you too will be encouraged when together you reach for Jesus. Encourage your friends.

Whoever has the gift of encouraging others should encourage. Whoever has the gift of giving to others should give freely. Anyone who has the gift of being a leader should try hard when he leads. Whoever has the gift of showing mercy to others should do so with joy.

ROMANS 12:8

. . .

So encourage each other and give each other strength, just as you are doing now.

1 THESSALONIANS 5:11

. . .

But encourage each other every day while it is "today." Help each other so none of you will become hardened because sin has tricked you.

HEBREWS 3:13

. . .

Let us think about each other and help each other to show love and do good deeds.

HEBREWS 10:24

7

BE WITHOUT PREJUDICE.

Always be unbiased, not just when it serves you well. To be prejudiced is not only unjust but also unfair. Look to the interests of all others; earn respect for your impartial, equitable character rather than contempt for your unfair and biased ways. Be without prejudice.

God makes people right with himself through their faith in Jesus Christ. This is true for all who believe in Christ, because all people are the same.

Romans 3:22

. . .

Do not be interested only in your own life, but be interested in the lives of others.

Philippians 2:4

. . .

Before God and Christ Jesus and the chosen angels, I command you to do these things without showing favor of any kind to anyone.

1 Timothy 5:21

. . .

My dear brothers and sisters, as believers in our glorious Lord Jesus Christ, never think some people are more important than others.

James 2:1

. . .

But if you treat one person as being more important than another, you are sinning. You are guilty of breaking God's law.

James 2:9

8

Offer your shoulder.

Be there, even if you haven't been asked to show up. When you are least expected is often when you are most needed. Giving comfort secures more real happiness than receiving, and besides, it is godlike and blesses forever. Offer your shoulder.

Come to me, all you who are weary and burdened,
and I will give you rest. Take my yoke upon you
and learn from me, for I am gentle and humble in
heart, and you will find rest for your souls. For my
yoke is easy and my burden is light.

MATTHEW 11:28–30 NIV

. . .

When the Lord saw her, he felt very sorry
for her and said, "Don't cry."

LUKE 7:13

. . .

[God] comforts us every time we have trouble,
so when others have trouble, we can comfort
them with the same comfort God gives us.

2 CORINTHIANS 1:4

. . .

But now you should forgive him and comfort him to
keep him from having too much sadness and giving
up completely. So I beg you to show that you love him.

2 CORINTHIANS 2:7–8

9

LIFT OTHERS UP.

Do not walk past and ignore someone who is down, but reach out your hand and take him into your heart. Be kind and compassionate to one another, just as in Christ God has been kind and compassionate to you. Your duty to others is illustrated by the example of Christ. He forgot himself in his work of saving men. You should too. Lift others up.

Love your neighbor as you love yourself.

LUKE 10:27

• • •

*Live in harmony with one another. Do not be proud,
but be willing to associate with people of low
position. Do not be conceited.*

ROMANS 12:16 NIV

• • •

*We who are strong in faith ought to bear with the failings
of the weak and not to please ourselves. Each of us should
please his neighbor for his good, to build him up.*

ROMANS 15:1–2 NIV

• • •

*Does your life in Christ give you strength? Does his
love comfort you? Do we share together in the spirit?
Do you have mercy and kindness? If so, make me
very happy by having the same thoughts, sharing
the same love, and having one mind and purpose.*

PHILIPPIANS 2:1–2

10

Be not indifferent.

With wisdom, there is also found humility, mercy, consideration, and love. Be not indifferent, but be wise and ready to do whatever is good and right, including loving those who may seem impossible to love. Christ died not only for his friends but for his enemies as well because he loved them too. Be not indifferent.

This is my command: Love each other as I have loved you.

JOHN 15:12

. . .

May the patience and encouragement that come from God allow you to live in harmony with each other the way Christ Jesus wants. Then you will all be joined together, and you will give glory to God the Father of our Lord Jesus Christ. Christ accepted you, so you should accept each other, which will bring glory to God.

ROMANS 15:5–7

. . .

Remind the believers to yield to the authority of rulers and government leaders, to obey them, to be ready to do good, to speak no evil about anyone, to live in peace, and to be gentle and polite to all people.

TITUS 3:1–2

. . .

But the wisdom that comes from God is first of all pure, then peaceful, gentle, and easy to please. This wisdom is always ready to help those who are troubled and to do good for others. It is always fair and honest.

JAMES 3:17

11

LEND HELPING HANDS.

Honest labor is the best remedy for a dishonest life. Every man is to work so that he might provide for himself and be able to help others. To do something for someone in need is pleasing to Christ. When you do, your faith will grow and be witnessed by many. That pleases Christ too. Lend helping hands.

Share with God's people who need help. Bring strangers in need into your homes.

Romans 12:13

. . .

Each of you should give as you have decided in your heart to give. You should not be sad when you give, and you should not give because you feel forced to give. God loves the person who gives happily.

2 Corinthians 9:7

. . .

Those who are stealing must stop stealing and start working. They should earn an honest living for themselves. Then they will have something to share with those who are poor.

Ephesians 4:28

. . .

A brother or sister in Christ might need clothes or food. If you say to that person, "God be with you! I hope you stay warm and get plenty to eat," but you do not give what that person needs, your words are worth nothing.

James 2:15–16

12

Ease others' burdens.

Life holds many burdens: financial, spiritual, emotional, and physical. To the extent you are able, help lighten others' burdens. Keep in mind that you yourself are not infallible or without fault, so judge others' circumstances gently. Ease others' burdens.

The only thing they asked us was to remember to help the poor—something I really wanted to do.

GALATIANS 2:10

. . .

By helping each other with your troubles, you truly obey the law of Christ.

GALATIANS 6:2

. . .

But it was good that you helped me when I needed it.

PHILIPPIANS 4:14

. . .

Tell the rich people to do good, to be rich in doing good deeds, to be generous and ready to share. By doing that, they will be saving a treasure for themselves as a strong foundation for the future. Then they will be able to have the life that is true life.

1 TIMOTHY 6:18–19

. . .

God is fair; he will not forget the work you did and the love you showed for him by helping his people. And he will remember that you are still helping them.

HEBREWS 6:10

13

LISTEN WITH UNDERSTANDING.

Pray that you might faithfully hear the Word and use the Word to glorify God in all other things that you hear and say. When listening to man, *what* you hear depends on *how* you hear. You should be quick to listen, but slow to speak and even slower to become angry (James 1:19), for anger does not bring about the Christian example that God desires. Listen with understanding.

Be happy with those who are happy,
and be sad with those who are sad.

. . .

Everything that is hidden will become clear, and
every secret thing will be made known. So be
careful how you listen. Those who have
understanding will be given more. But those who do
not have understanding, even what they think they
have will be taken away from them.

LUKE 8:17–18

. . .

And a servant of the Lord must not quarrel but must
be kind to everyone, a good teacher, and patient.
The Lord's servant must gently teach those who
disagree. Then maybe God will let them change
their minds so they can accept the truth.

2 TIMOTHY 2:24–25

. . .

My dear brothers and sisters, always be willing to listen and
slow to speak. Do not become angry easily, because anger
will not help you live the right kind of life God wants.

JAMES 1:19–20

14

Tell the truth.

Simply let your yes be yes and your no be no. You are a member of the Christian household, and every member has a right to the truth; do not lie. Have faith, and trust the results of honoring and defending the truth. Turn away from your former ill practices and conduct yourself as a new and better person. Tell the truth.

Say only yes if you mean yes, and no if you mean no. If you say more than yes or no, it is from the Evil One.

MATTHEW 5:37

. . .

So you must stop telling lies. Tell each other the truth, because we all belong to each other in the same body. When you are angry, do not sin, and be sure to stop being angry before the end of the day. Do not give the devil a way to defeat you.

EPHESIANS 4:25–27

. . .

But now also put these things out of your life: anger, bad temper, doing or saying things to hurt others, and using evil words when you talk. Do not lie to each other. You have left your old sinful life and the things you did before.

COLOSSIANS 3:8–9

. . .

The Scripture says, "A person must do these things to enjoy life and have many happy days. He must not say evil things, and he must not tell lies. He must stop doing evil and do good. He must look for peace and work for it."

1 PETER 3:10–11

15

USE MEASURED WORDS.

Words can be either lasting solace or lethal poison. The good man brings good things out of the good stored up in him, and the evil man brings evil things out of the evil stored up in him. Do not utter both blessing and cursing, good and evil, for such contradictions only insult God and discourage his people. Think before speaking. Use measured words.

Good people have good things in their hearts, and so they say good things. But evil people have evil in their hearts, so they say evil things. And I tell you that on the Judgment Day people will be responsible for every careless thing they have said. The words you have said will be used to judge you. Some of your words will prove you right, but some of your words will prove you guilty.

MATTHEW 12:35–37

. . .

Besides that, they learn to waste their time, going from house to house. And they not only waste their time but also begin to gossip and busy themselves with other people's lives, saying things they should not say.

1 TIMOTHY 5:13

. . .

We use our tongues to praise our Lord and Father, but then we curse people, whom God made like himself. Praises and curses come from the same mouth! My brothers and sisters, this should not happen.

JAMES 3:9–10

16

Do good deeds.

The call to all Christians is to do good deeds; by your good deeds you bring glory to God. Your faith in God—if that faith is without good deeds—is not enough. Care for others and encourage them to do their own good deeds, all wrapped in love, for that love identifies you as a faithful child of God. Do good deeds.

In the same way, you should be a light for other people. Live so that they will see the good things you do and will praise your Father in heaven.

MATTHEW 5:16

. . .

We must not become tired of doing good. We will receive our harvest of eternal life at the right time if we do not give up. When we have the opportunity to help anyone, we should do it. But we should give special attention to those who are in the family of believers.

GALATIANS 6:9–10

. . .

This is my prayer for you: that your love will grow more and more; that you will have knowledge and understanding with your love; that you will see the difference between good and bad and will choose the good; that you will be pure and without wrong for the coming of Christ.

PHILIPPIANS 1:9–10

. . .

My children, we should love people not only with words and talk, but by our actions and true caring.

1 JOHN 3:18

17

Act with mercy.

Mercy begets mercy, and the lack of mercy earns you nothing. Be gentle to those who are disturbed by doubt or who have wronged you. If you are hard and unforgiving toward others, you can never expect God to forgive your sins. The nature of your mind toward others determines the nature of God's mind toward you. Act with mercy.

They are blessed who show mercy to others,
for God will show mercy to them.

MATTHEW 5:7

. . .

Then the master called his servant in and said, "You
evil servant! Because you begged me to forget what
you owed, I told you that you did not have to pay
anything. You should have showed mercy to that
other servant, just as I showed mercy to you."

MATTHEW 18:32–33

. . .

Be merciful, just as your Father is merciful.

LUKE 6:36 NIV

. . .

So you must show mercy to others, or God will not show
mercy to you when he judges you. But the person who
shows mercy can stand without fear at the judgment.

JAMES 2:13

18

Help others succeed.

If Christ encourages and blesses you, follow his example! Serve not only your own interests but also the interests of others, all the while urging them on toward their own good deeds, not letting them fall into confusion or failure. Help others succeed.

I planted the seed, and Apollos watered it. But God is the One who made it grow. So the one who plants is not important, and the one who waters is not important. Only God, who makes things grow, is important. The one who plants and the one who waters have the same purpose, and each will be rewarded for his own work.

1 Corinthians 3:6–8

. . .

We do not want you to have troubles while other people are at ease, but we want everything to be equal. At this time you have plenty. What you have can help others who are in need. Then later, when they have plenty, they can help you when you are in need, and all will be equal. As it is written in the Scriptures, "The person who gathered more did not have too much, nor did the person who gathered less have too little."

2 Corinthians 8:13–15

. . .

When you do things, do not let selfishness or pride be your guide. Instead, be humble and give more honor to others than to yourselves. Do not be interested only in your own life, but be interested in the lives of others.

Philippians 2:3–4

19

CHERISH YOUR SPOUSE.

Marriage is a relationship of mutual obligations. Each spouse must offer to the other what those obligations require. Your spouse is a great blessing given to you so that you may more fully enjoy your life. Honor and treasure that blessing. You are called to love your spouse just as Christ loved the church, with loving devotion and lifelong fidelity (Ephesians 5:25). Cherish your spouse.

And God said, "So a man will leave his father and mother and be united with his wife, and the two will become one body." So there are not two, but one. God has joined the two together, so no one should separate them.

MATTHEW 19:5–6

. . .

The husband should give his wife all that he owes her as his wife. And the wife should give her husband all that she owes him as her husband. The wife does not have full rights over her own body; her husband shares them. And the husband does not have full rights over his own body; his wife shares them.

1 CORINTHIANS 7:3–4

. . .

Love suffers long and is kind; love does not envy; love does not parade itself, is not puffed up; does not behave rudely, does not seek its own, is not provoked, thinks no evil; does not rejoice in iniquity, but rejoices in the truth; bears all things, believes all things, hopes all things, endures all things.

1 CORINTHIANS 13:4–7 NKJV

20

Love your neighbor.

You may commit acts of charity and kindness, but unless your acts are motivated by love, your good deeds mean nothing in the eyes of the Lord. By loving your neighbor, you continue Christ's work of spreading the hope of salvation and everlasting life. Be a disciple; love others so well that there will be mutual regard and affection, all for God's greater glory. Love your neighbor.

*This is the teaching you have heard from the
beginning: We must love each other.*

1 JOHN 3:11

. . .

*I give you a new command: Love each other. You must
love each other as I have loved you. All people will know
that you are my followers if you love each other.*

JOHN 13:34–35

. . .

*You did not choose me; I chose you. And I gave you
this work: to go and produce fruit, fruit that will last.
Then the Father will give you anything you ask for
in my name. This is my command: Love each other.*

JOHN 15:16–17

. . .

*I may speak in different languages of people or even angels. But
if I do not have love, I am only a noisy bell or a crashing cymbal.
I may have the gift of prophecy. I may understand all the secret
things of God and have all knowledge, and I may have faith so
great I can move mountains. But even with all these things, if I
do not have love, then I am nothing. I may give away everything
I have, and I may even give my body as an offering to be
burned. But I gain nothing if I do not have love.*

1 CORINTHIANS 13:1–3

21

LOVE THE UNLOVED.

Take great care not to befriend only those in prosperous and influential places. Remember that Jesus dined with and cared for the outcast, instead of staying only in the company of the king's court and temple priests. If you enjoy the love of Christ, you must share your blessings and faithfully care for the poor and downtrodden. Having contempt for anyone only encourages the nonbeliever. Love the unloved.

*Be careful. Don't think these little children are worth
nothing. I tell you that they have angels in heaven
who are always with my Father in heaven.*

MATTHEW 18:10

. . .

*Then the King will answer, "I tell you the truth, anything you
did for even the least of my people here, you also did for me."*

MATTHEW 25:40

. . .

*Then the King will answer, "I tell you the truth,
anything you refused to do for even the least of my
people here, you refused to do for me."*

MATTHEW 25:45

. . .

*Always be humble, gentle, and patient,
accepting each other in love.*

EPHESIANS 4:2

. . .

*People will no longer have to teach their neighbors
and relatives to know the Lord, because all people
will know me, from the least to the most important.*

HEBREWS 8:11

22

Love your enemies.

Not one of us is deserving of God's compassion, yet we are forgiven. Christ on the cross prayed for his enemies; so did Stephen, the first Christian martyr. If someone does you wrong, remember Christ's example. Just as God loves you, you should love your enemies, forgiving them for their offenses against you. When you do, you give glory to God by multiplying his forgiveness. Love your enemies.

*Wish good for those who harm you; wish
them well and do not curse them.*

ROMANS 12:14

. . .

*You have heard that it was said, "Love your neighbor and
hate your enemies." But I say to you, love your enemies.
Pray for those who hurt you. If you do this, you will be true
children of your Father in heaven. He causes the sun to
rise on good people and on evil people, and he sends rain
to those who do right and to those who do wrong.*

MATTHEW 5:43–45

. . .

*But I say to you who are listening, love your enemies.
Do good to those who hate you, bless those who curse
you, pray for those who are cruel to you.*

LUKE 6:27–28

. . .

*But love your enemies, do good to them, and lend to them
without hoping to get anything back. Then you will have a
great reward, and you will be children of the Most High God,
because he is kind even to people who are ungrateful and
full of sin. Show mercy, just as your Father shows mercy.*

LUKE 6:35–36

23

DO NO HARM.

Christ suffered the punishment of our sins so that we might be reconciled with God. All he asks in return is that we obey the new law: to love one another. Love is compassionate and kind, not harmful. Don't let the fact that you were treated wrongly cause you to commit another wrong. Instead, overcome evil with love, mercy, and restraint. Do no harm.

If someone does wrong to you, do not pay him back by doing wrong to him. Try to do what everyone thinks is right. Do your best to live in peace with everyone.

Romans 12:17–18

. . .

Love never hurts a neighbor, so loving is obeying all the law.

Romans 13:10

. . .

Do not be bitter or angry or mad. Never shout angrily or say things to hurt others. Never do anything evil.

Ephesians 4:31

. . .

This is what you were called to do, because Christ suffered for you and gave you an example to follow. So you should do as he did. "He had never sinned, and he had never lied." People insulted Christ, but he did not insult them in return. Christ suffered, but he did not threaten. He let God, the One who judges rightly, take care of him.

1 Peter 2:21–23

24

Count to three.

Counting to three implies self-control. Self-control refers to control of not only the temper but also the tongue and passion for money or power. Be careful not to act or speak rashly, especially in anger. Under the influence of anger, you are easily tempted to commit evil and display something very different from God's righteousness. If Christ is your example, self-control must be found in you. Count to three.

And do not make the Holy Spirit sad. The Spirit is God's proof that you belong to him. God gave you the Spirit to show that God will make you free when the final day comes. Do not be bitter or angry or mad. Never shout angrily or say things to hurt others. Never do anything evil.

EPHESIANS 4:30–31

. . .

The purpose of this command is for people to have love, a love that comes from a pure heart and a good conscience and a true faith. Some people have missed these things and turned to useless talk. They want to be teachers of the law, but they do not understand either what they are talking about or what they are sure about.

1 TIMOTHY 1:5–7

. . .

For the grace of God that brings salvation has appeared to all men. It teaches us to say "No" to ungodliness and worldly passions, and to live self-controlled, upright and godly lives in this present age.

TITUS 2:11–12 NIV

25

CALM TROUBLED WATERS.

Live and encourage peaceful lives. Christ understood that for the gospel to be made known, believers must be peace-loving rather than quarrelsome so that those who had not yet heard the Word would listen rather than turn away. Don't participate in or encourage foolish and stupid arguments that lead to conflict rather than peace. Calm troubled waters.

So let us try to do what makes peace and helps one another.

ROMANS 14:19

. . .

So, I want the men everywhere to pray, lifting up their hands in a holy manner, without anger and arguments.

1 TIMOTHY 2:8

. . .

And a servant of the Lord must not quarrel but must be kind to everyone, a good teacher, and patient. The Lord's servant must gently teach those who disagree. Then maybe God will let them change their minds so they can accept the truth.

2 TIMOTHY 2:24–25

. . .

But the wisdom that comes from God is first of all pure, then peaceful, gentle, and easy to please. This wisdom is always ready to help those who are troubled and to do good for others. It is always fair and honest. People who work for peace in a peaceful way plant a good crop of right-living.

JAMES 3:17–18

26

Act with compassion.

Jesus had compassion with everyone, attending first to their worldly hunger and thirst and then to their spiritual deprivation. Acts of compassion demonstrate the unfailing concern Christ has for the people, his sheep. In this way you will also become a shepherd. Act with compassion.

If a person asks you for something, give it to him. Don't refuse to give to someone who wants to borrow from you.

MATTHEW 5:42

. . .

When [Jesus] arrived, he saw a great crowd waiting. He felt sorry for them, because they were like sheep without a shepherd. So he began to teach them many things.

MARK 6:34

. . .

Then Jesus said to the man who had invited him, "When you give a lunch or a dinner, don't invite only your friends, your family, your other relatives, and your rich neighbors. At another time they will invite you to eat with them, and you will be repaid. Instead, when you give a feast, invite the poor, the crippled, the lame, and the blind. Then you will be blessed, because they have nothing and cannot pay you back. But you will be repaid when the good people rise from the dead."

LUKE 14:12–14

27

Walk straight paths.

All that is good lies along the straight path. It is on the dark, meandering trail that wickedness and deceit are found. Pay attention not only to what Jesus taught but also how he lived. Rise above slander and spite; live your life in the service of God, relying on the truth of the Word as your daily guide. Walk straight paths.

*Brothers and sisters, think about the things that are
good and worthy of praise. Think about the things that
are true and honorable and right and pure and beautiful
and respected. Do what you learned and received from
me, what I told you, and what you saw me do. And the
God who gives peace will be with you.*

PHILIPPIANS 4:8–9

. . .

*[Grace] teaches us not to live against God nor to
do the evil things the world wants to do. Instead,
that grace teaches us to live in the present age in
a wise and right way and in a way that shows we
serve God. We should live like that while we wait
for our great hope and the coming of the glory of
our great God and Savior Jesus Christ.*

TITUS 2:12–13

. . .

*So then, rid yourselves of all evil, all lying, hypocrisy,
jealousy, and evil speech. As newborn babies want milk,
you should want the pure and simple teaching. By it you
can mature in your salvation, because you have already
examined and seen how good the Lord is.*

1 PETER 2:1–3

28

OVERCOME YOUR DOUBT.

Jesus said that if you believe, you will receive whatever you ask for in prayer. He also said not to be afraid, just believe. Set aside worldly reason and believe the Word. When you do, your eyes will be opened and your heart renewed. Overcome your doubt.

If you believe, you will get anything you ask for in prayer.

Matthew 21:22

. . .

Faith means being sure of the things we hope for and knowing that something is real even if we do not see it. Faith is the reason we remember great people who lived in the past. It is by faith we understand that the whole world was made by God's command so what we see was made by something that cannot be seen.

Hebrews 11:1–3

. . .

But when you ask God, you must believe and not doubt. Anyone who doubts is like a wave in the sea, blown up and down by the wind. Such doubters are thinking two different things at the same time, and they cannot decide about anything they do. They should not think they will receive anything from the Lord.

James 1:6–8

. . .

Show mercy to some people who have doubts. Take others out of the fire, and save them. Show mercy mixed with fear to others, hating even their clothes which are dirty from sin.

Jude vv. 22–23

29

Strive for justice.

Seek justice not only for yourself but also for everyone. It is in seeking justice for all that you please the Lord, showing your love and regard for your neighbors and your equal dislike of favoritism, deceit, and exploitation. Strive for justice.

*Stop judging by the way things look, but
judge by what is really right.*

JOHN 7:24

. . .

*Peter began to speak: "I really understand now that to God
every person is the same. In every country God accepts
anyone who worships him and does what is right."*

ACTS 10:34–35

. . .

*You pray to God and call him Father, and he judges
each person's work equally. So while you are here on
earth, you should live with respect for God.*

1 PETER 1:17

. . .

*So we can see who God's children are and who the
devil's children are: Those who do not do what is right
are not God's children, and those who do not love
their brothers and sisters are not God's children.*

1 JOHN 3:10

30

Act with tenderness.

Opposers of the Word must be corrected, not rudely but instead gently, kindly, humbly. Jesus' tenderness drew people to him. In his gentle company, they stopped and listened to his message. Be like-minded, and be heard. Act with tenderness.

Does your life in Christ give you strength? Does his love comfort you? Do we share together in the spirit? Do you have mercy and kindness? If so, make me very happy by having the same thoughts, sharing the same love, and having one mind and purpose.

P‍HILIPPIANS 2:1–2

. . .

And a servant of the Lord must not quarrel but must be kind to everyone, a good teacher, and patient.

2 T‍IMOTHY 2:24

. . .

People who think they are religious but say things they should not say are just fooling themselves. Their "religion" is worth nothing.

J‍AMES 1:26

. . .

Are there those among you who are truly wise and understanding? Then they should show it by living right and doing good things with a gentleness that comes from wisdom.

J‍AMES 3:13

31

DO YOUR BEST.

In all that you do you are a representative of Christ; therefore, in whatever you do, do it with all your heart to honor Christ and his message. To this end, spare no time, self-denial, or effort, for it pleases the Lord when you do your good deeds often and well. If you render good service anywhere to anyone, the Lord will see that you are rewarded. Do your best.

You know that in a race all the runners run, but only one gets the prize. So run to win! All those who compete in the games use self-control so they can win a crown. That crown is an earthly thing that lasts only a short time, but our crown will never be destroyed.

1 Corinthians 9:24–25

· · ·

Do your work with enthusiasm. Work as if you were serving the Lord, not as if you were serving only men and women.

Ephesians 6:7

· · ·

In all the work you are doing, work the best you can. Work as if you were doing it for the Lord, not for people.

Colossians 3:23

· · ·

Make every effort to give yourself to God as the kind of person he will approve. Be a worker who is not ashamed and who uses the true teaching in the right way.

2 Timothy 2:15

32

Share your blessings.

The Lord gave himself for you; what shall you give for him? All that you have is not your own but was provided to you by God. Make the needs of others your own and help them, giving freely and cheerfully in order to be blessed. Share what he has given you, and in the process, please and honor him who has made you rich in heaven. Giving for God's purposes are indeed sacrifices that please him. Share your blessings.

Do not forget to do good to others, and share with them, because such sacrifices please God.

HEBREWS 13:16

. . .

John answered, "If you have two shirts, share with the person who does not have one. If you have food, share that also."

LUKE 3:11

. . .

You are rich in everything—in faith, in speaking, in knowledge, in truly wanting to help, and in the love you learned from us. In the same way, be strong also in the grace of giving. I am not commanding you to give. But I want to see if your love is true by comparing you with others that really want to help. You know the grace of our Lord Jesus Christ. You know that Christ was rich, but for you he became poor so that by his becoming poor you might become rich.

2 CORINTHIANS 8:7–9

33

REFRAIN FROM REVENGE.

Justice belongs only to the sovereign Lord. Do not make it your business to judge and avenge, for as you judge, you too will be judged. Rid yourself of a wrathful mind. If it is possible, as far as you have any say or influence in the matter, live at peace with everyone (Romans 12:18). Refrain from revenge.

If you go on hurting each other and tearing each other apart, be careful, or you will completely destroy each other.

GALATIANS 5:15

. . .

Be sure that no one pays back wrong for wrong, but always try to do what is good for each other and for all people.

1 THESSALONIANS 5:15

. . .

We know that God said, "I will punish those who do wrong; I will repay them." And he also said, "The Lord will judge his people."

HEBREWS 10:30

. . .

Do not do wrong to repay a wrong, and do not insult to repay an insult. But repay with a blessing, because you yourselves were called to do this so that you might receive a blessing.

1 PETER 3:9

34

Swallow your pride.

Although he was from most high, Jesus spent time with the lowest of the low, showing that his mercy and grace are for all. Let there be harmony and a spirit of agreement wherever you go, for the way to secure grace more abundantly is to be humble before the Lord. Be humble with others, just as Jesus is with you. Swallow your pride.

Live in peace with each other. Do not be proud, but make friends with those who seem unimportant. Do not think how smart you are.

ROMANS 12:16

. . .

Love is patient and kind. Love is not jealous, it does not brag, and it is not proud.

1 CORINTHIANS 13:4

. . .

When you do things, do not let selfishness or pride be your guide. Instead, be humble and give more honor to others than to yourselves.

PHILIPPIANS 2:3

. . .

But God gives us even more grace, as the Scripture says, "God is against the proud, but he gives grace to the humble."

JAMES 4:6

35

LIVE IN PEACE.

You are called to be a peacemaker. If you are filled with the love of peace, it must reign in your heart and then rule in your deeds. There must be no disagreement, separation, or rebellion between you and your neighbors, for without peace no one will see the Lord. Being agreeable allows others to see God at work through you. Live in peace.

Do your best to live in peace with everyone.

ROMANS 12:18

. . .

*So let us try to do what makes peace
and helps one another.*

ROMANS 14:19

. . .

*Let the peace that Christ gives control your
thinking, because you were all called together in
one body to have peace. Always be thankful.*

COLOSSIANS 3:15

. . .

*Try to live in peace with all people, and try to
live free from sin. Anyone whose life is not
holy will never see the Lord.*

HEBREWS 12:14

36

Ask for forgiveness.

If we confess our sins, the Lord will be faithful to his promise of mercy (1 John 1:9). We all need forgiveness and healing. Confess your faults as a demonstration of repentance. Repentance is not sorrow, but the fruit of sorrow. It is an internal change resulting not from remorse but from conviction of sin and sincere sorrow for it. Not one of us is without sin; our mistakes are many. Confess your sins to God and man so that you might be cleansed, forgiven, and healed. Ask for forgiveness.

Confess your sins to each other and pray for each other so God can heal you. When a believing person prays, great things happen.

JAMES 5:16

. . .

Peter said to them, "Change your hearts and lives and be baptized, each one of you, in the name of Jesus Christ for the forgiveness of your sins. And you will receive the gift of the Holy Spirit."

ACTS 2:38

. . .

So you must change your hearts and lives! Come back to God, and he will forgive your sins. Then the Lord will send the time of rest.

ACTS 3:19

. . .

If we say we have no sin, we are fooling ourselves, and the truth is not in us. But if we confess our sins, he will forgive our sins, because we can trust God to do what is right. He will cleanse us from all the wrongs we have done.

1 JOHN 1:8–9

37

FORGIVE ALL WRONGS.

You cannot be forgiven without also being one who can forgive. To obtain our forgiveness, our Lord makes it a condition that we have a merciful spirit as well. You are to forgive others for their wrongs in the same way that God forgives yours; mercy must not be refused if someone comes to you in the spirit of sincere repentance. Forgive all wrongs.

Yes, if you forgive others for their sins, your Father in heaven will also forgive you for your sins. But if you don't forgive others, your Father in heaven will not forgive your sins.

MATTHEW 6:14–15

. . .

When you are praying, if you are angry with someone, forgive him so that your Father in heaven will also forgive your sins.

MARK 11:25

. . .

But now you should forgive him and comfort him to keep him from having too much sadness and giving up completely. So I beg you to show that you love him.

2 CORINTHIANS 2:7–8

. . .

Be kind and loving to each other, and forgive each other just as God forgave you in Christ.

EPHESIANS 4:32

. . .

Bear with each other, and forgive each other. If someone does wrong to you, forgive that person because the Lord forgave you.

COLOSSIANS 3:13

38

Forgive yourself too.

Is your standard higher than Christ's? You, forgiven through him, are made righteous before God and cannot be under condemnation, even of your own judgment. With your faith in him, he has forgiven you, so forgive yourself so that his grace may be glorified and his good name proclaimed for all to hear. Forgive yourself too.

*Therefore, my brothers, I want you to know that through
Jesus the forgiveness of sins is proclaimed to you.*

. . .

*Therefore, there is now no condemnation for those who are
in Christ Jesus, because through Christ Jesus the law of the
Spirit of life set me free from the law of sin and death.*

ROMANS 8:1–2 NIV

. . .

*I will forgive them for the wicked things they did,
and I will not remember their sins anymore.*

HEBREWS 8:12

. . .

*This is the way we know that we belong to the way
of truth. When our hearts make us feel guilty, we
can still have peace before God. God is greater than
our hearts, and he knows everything. My dear
friends, if our hearts do not make us feel guilty, we
can come without fear into God's presence. And
God gives us what we ask for because we obey
God's commands and do what pleases him.*

1 JOHN 3:19–22

39

ACKNOWLEDGE YOUR WEAKNESSES.

The body is weak; guard against its temptation with prayer, relying on Christ's strength and giving him praise for his power. Christ not only strengthens you, but—even in your weakness and imperfection—he also continues to love you as you rely more heavily on him. With your confession, you will grow strong. Acknowledge your weaknesses.

*Watch and pray so that you will not fall into
temptation. The spirit is willing, but the body is weak.*

MATTHEW 26:41 NIV

. . .

*Also, the Spirit helps us with our weakness. We do
not know how to pray as we should. But the Spirit
himself speaks to God for us, even begs God for us
with deep feelings that words cannot explain.*

ROMANS 8:26

. . .

*I begged the Lord three times to take this problem
away from me. But he said to me, "My grace is
enough for you. When you are weak, my power is
made perfect in you." So I am very happy to brag
about my weaknesses. Then Christ's power can live
in me. For this reason I am happy when I have
weaknesses, insults, hard times, sufferings, and all
kinds of troubles for Christ. Because when I am
weak, then I am truly strong.*

2 CORINTHIANS 12:8–10

40

Live as servants.

Even the Son of man did not come to be served, but to serve and to give his life as a ransom for many (Matthew 20:28). Be a shepherd of God's flock; give an example that others may follow, not because you must but because you are willing and eager to serve, just as Jesus serves as your shepherd. Christ will see and reward your good deeds. Even if you receive no earthly rewards, you will indeed prosper in spirit. Live as servants.

Those who give one of these little ones a cup of cold water because they are my followers will truly get their reward.

MATTHEW 10:42

. . .

In the same way, the Son of Man did not come to be served. He came to serve others and to give his life as a ransom for many people.

MARK 10:45

. . .

Though I am free and belong to no man, I make myself a slave to everyone, to win as many as possible.

1 CORINTHIANS 9:19 NIV

. . .

My brothers and sisters, God called you to be free, but do not use your freedom as an excuse to do what pleases your sinful self. Serve each other with love.

GALATIANS 5:13

. . .

Live as free people, but do not use your freedom as an excuse to do evil. Live as servants of God.

1 PETER 2:16

41

OVERCOME YOUR TRIALS.

Even though your body may waste away under painful trials or be threatened with death, your spiritual strength can be constantly renewed by Christ. Trials remind you of your dependence on God. Give in to your trials, and you begin to turn away from him, but remain faithful and pray to the Lord, and your appeals will be heard. You—and your faith—will be strengthened as a result. Overcome your trials.

My brothers and sisters, when you ha[v]
kinds of troubles, you should be full
because you know that these troubles t
faith, and this will give you patien[c]

James 1:2–3

. . .

We have small troubles for a while now, but they are
helping us gain an eternal glory that is much greater
than the troubles. We set our eyes not on what we see
but on what we cannot see. What we see will last only a
short time, but what we cannot see will last forever.

2 Corinthians 4:17–18

. . .

So hold on through your sufferings, because they are
like a father's discipline. God is treating you as
children. All children are disciplined by their fathers.

Hebrews 12:7

. . .

A person might have to suffer even when it is unfair, but
if he thinks of God and stands the pain, God is pleased.

1 Peter 2:19

42

Strive for congruence.

The evidence that you have a saving knowledge of Christ is loyal obedience to his commandments. Don't be the one who speaks of yourself in holy terms but then walks in dark, lowly places. A profession of faith joined with a wicked life leads no one to the Lord. Do not contradict your words with your deeds and distract from the work you are called to accomplish. If you abide in Christ, live as he did. Practice what you preach. Strive for congruence.

Now that you are obedient children of God do not live as you did in the past. You did not understand, so you did the evil things you wanted. But be holy in all you do, just as God, the One who called you, is holy. It is written in the Scriptures: "You must be holy, because I am holy."

1 PETER 1:14–16

. . .

So if we say we have fellowship with God, but we continue living in darkness, we are liars and do not follow the truth.

1 JOHN 1:6

. . .

We can be sure that we know God if we obey his commands. Anyone who says, "I know God," but does not obey God's commands is a liar, and the truth is not in that person. But if someone obeys God's teaching, then in that person God's love has truly reached its goal. This is how we can be sure we are living in God: Whoever says that he lives in God must live as Jesus lived.

1 JOHN 2:3–6

43

ACT WITH HUMILITY.

You are a representative of Christ; your actions should reflect positively on him. You are not forbidden from behaving righteously before men but from making it your goal to be seen for the sake of receiving their praise. Do nothing for your own glory, for you cannot save yourself. Jesus has done that work for you. Therefore, bring glory to him; represent him well. Act with humility.

Be careful! When you do good things, don't do them in front of people to be seen by them. If you do that, you will have no reward from your Father in heaven. . . . So when you give to the poor, don't let anyone know what you are doing. Your giving should be done in secret. Your Father can see what is done in secret, and he will reward you.

MATTHEW 6:1, 3–4

. . .

We must not be proud or make trouble with each other or be jealous of each other.

GALATIANS 5:26

. . .

When you do things, do not let selfishness or pride be your guide. Instead, be humble and give more honor to others than to yourselves.

PHILIPPIANS 2:3

. . .

In the same way, younger people should be willing to be under older people. And all of you should be very humble with each other. "God is against the proud, but he gives grace to the humble." Be humble under God's powerful hand so he will lift you up when the right time comes.

1 PETER 5:5–6

44

Honor your body.

Your body is mortal and will be conquered by death, but it must not be conquered by sin and used as a pawn of evil. If the Holy Spirit dwells in you, your body is his. Treat your body respectfully and morally, and with it do righteous deeds so that Christ might reside within a holy host. Honor your body.

Do not offer the parts of your body to serve sin, as things to be used in doing evil. Instead, offer yourselves to God as people who have died and now live. Offer the parts of your body to God to be used in doing good.

ROMANS 6:13

. . .

I use this example because this is hard for you to understand. In the past you offered the parts of your body to be slaves to sin and evil; you lived only for evil. In the same way now you must give yourselves to be slaves of goodness. Then you will live only for God.

ROMANS 6:19

. . .

You should know that your body is a temple for the Holy Spirit who is in you. You have received the Holy Spirit from God. So you do not belong to yourselves, because you were bought by God for a price. So honor God with your bodies.

1 CORINTHIANS 6:19–20

. . .

God wants you to be holy and to stay away from sexual sins. He wants each of you to learn to control your own body in a way that is holy and honorable.

1 THESSALONIANS 4:3–4

45

SOFTEN YOUR HEART.

In your stubbornness you refuse the Lord, but in your submissiveness you trust in him who is merciful and just. Do not love the world and its distractions and make your guilt and condemnation greater. Instead, turn away from sin and come to Christ with a broken and remorseful spirit, and you will be healed. Soften your heart.

*For the minds of these people have become
stubborn. They do not hear with their ears, and they
have closed their eyes. Otherwise they might really
understand what they see with their eyes and hear
with their ears. They might really understand in
their minds and come back to me and be healed.*

MATTHEW 13:15

· · ·

*But you are stubborn and refuse to change, so you are making
your own punishment even greater on the day he shows his
anger. On that day everyone will see God's right judgments.*

ROMANS 2:5

· · ·

*I pray also that you will have greater understanding in
your heart so you will know the hope to which he has
called us and that you will know how rich and glorious
are the blessings God has promised his holy people.*

EPHESIANS 1:18

· · ·

*So brothers and sisters, be careful that none
of you has an evil, unbelieving heart that will
turn you away from the living God.*

HEBREWS 3:12

46

Share your joy.

To share your joy with others, to love others as Jesus loves you, is not only a form of thanksgiving and praise but also a way to cause others to wonder what you are so happy about. If you are moved by the power of faith and the constant comfort found in the presence of Christ, you should eagerly tell others about him. Share your joy.

*I have obeyed my Father's commands, and I remain in
his love. In the same way, if you obey my commands,
you will remain in my love. I have told you these
things so that you can have the same joy I have and
so that your joy will be the fullest possible joy.
This is my command: Love each other as I have loved you.*

John 15:10–12

. . .

*I am not ashamed of the Good News, because it is the
power God uses to save everyone who believes—to
save the Jews first, and then to save non-Jews.*

Romans 1:16

. . .

*It is written in the Scriptures, "I believed, so I spoke."
Our faith is like this, too. We believe, and so we speak.*

2 Corinthians 4:13

. . .

*I pray that the faith you share may make you
understand every blessing we have in Christ.*

Philemon v. 6

47

SAY THANK YOU.

Y ou should always be thankful because the Lord will always be with you and work all things together for your own good. Be thankful in all that you do and say, even if you must wait for what you seek, for in God you have already received the greatest gift: eternal life. Say thank you.

*As you received Christ Jesus the Lord, so continue
to live in him. Keep your roots deep in him and have
your lives built on him. Be strong in the faith, just as
you were taught, and always be thankful.*

COLOSSIANS 2:6–7

. . .

*Let the teaching of Christ live in you richly. Use all
wisdom to teach and instruct each other by singing
psalms, hymns, and spiritual songs with thankfulness
in your hearts to God. Everything you do or say should
be done to obey Jesus your Lord. And in all you do,
give thanks to God the Father through Jesus.*

COLOSSIANS 3:16–17

. . .

*Always be joyful. Pray continually, and give thanks whatever
happens. That is what God wants for you in Christ Jesus.*

1 THESSALONIANS 5:16–18

. . .

*So let us be thankful, because we have a kingdom
that cannot be shaken. We should worship God in a
way that pleases him with respect and fear.*

HEBREWS 12:28

48

Reward others first.

You should not first seek your own reward, but instead place the needs and interests of others before your own. Sacrifice for the benefit of others out of reverence for Christ, and give freely and unselfishly as he gave himself freely and unselfishly for you. Reward others first.

Do not look out only for yourselves. Look out for the good of others also.

1 Corinthians 10:24

. . .

Never do anything that might hurt others—Jews, Greeks, or God's church—just as I, also, try to please everybody in every way. I am not trying to do what is good for me but what is good for most people so they can be saved.

1 Corinthians 10:32–33

. . .

We must not be proud or make trouble with each other or be jealous of each other.

Galatians 5:26

. . .

When you do things, do not let selfishness or pride be your guide. Instead, be humble and give more honor to others than to yourselves.

Philippians 2:3

. . .

Where jealousy and selfishness are, there will be confusion and every kind of evil.

James 3:16

49

SERVE EACH OTHER.

Christ demonstrated his love by serving others, even offering his life to save yours. Greatness in the kingdom of heaven consists in doing rather than in being and in doing for others rather than for yourself. Greatness rises out of service. Only those who are the servants of mankind are truly great. Act as a child of God and rely on his strength. Serve others not only to honor Christ but also to continue his work of spreading the Word. Serve each other.

Whoever wants to become great among you must serve the rest of you like a servant. Whoever wants to become first among you must serve the rest of you like a slave. In the same way, the Son of Man did not come to be served. He came to serve others and to give his life as a ransom for many people.

MATTHEW 20:26–28

• • •

If I, your Lord and Teacher, have washed your feet, you also should wash each other's feet. I did this as an example so that you should do as I have done for you.

JOHN 13:14–15

• • •

You should produce much fruit and show that you are my followers, which brings glory to my Father.

JOHN 15:8

• • •

Each of you has received a gift to use to serve others. Be good servants of God's various gifts of grace.

1 PETER 4:10

50

Lead by example.

The business of the church is not only to save but also to enlighten. Christ is the light, and his disciples must also be light. To fit in with the crowd is to miss an opportunity to be an example of Jesus and show his goodness and mercy. Always reveal Christ by your words and deeds. Be a beacon; shine like stars so that others can see what you do for your Lord. Lead by example.

You are the light that gives light to the world. A city that is built on a hill cannot be hidden. And people don't hide a light under a bowl. They put it on a lampstand so the light shines for all the people in the house. In the same way, you should be a light for other people. Live so that they will see the good things you do and will praise your Father in heaven.

MATTHEW 5:14–16

. . .

But you are living with crooked and mean people all around you, among whom you shine like stars in the dark world.

PHILIPPIANS 2:15

. . .

Do not let anyone treat you as if you are unimportant because you are young. Instead, be an example to the believers with your words, your actions, your love, your faith, and your pure life.

1 TIMOTHY 4:12

. . .

People who do not believe are living all around you and might say that you are doing wrong. Live such good lives that they will see the good things you do and will give glory to God on the day when Christ comes again.

1 PETER 2:12

51

EMBRACE YOUR RESPONSIBILITY.

The work of evangelism is hard, but to shy away from it is to leave room for lies and chaos to fill the spaces where the truth should be. Boast of the Word and its teachings about Christ. Fear no evil, fight the good fight, and defend the truth. Embrace your responsibility.

I use this example because this is hard for you to understand. In the past you offered the parts of your body to be slaves to sin and evil; you lived only for evil. In the same way now you must give yourselves to be slaves of goodness. Then you will live only for God.

Romans 6:19

. . .

We ask you, brothers and sisters, to warn those who do not work. Encourage the people who are afraid. Help those who are weak. Be patient with everyone.

1 Thessalonians 5:14

. . .

But you, man of God, run away from all those things. Instead, live in the right way, serve God, have faith, love, patience, and gentleness. Fight the good fight of faith, grabbing hold of the life that continues forever. You were called to have that life when you confessed the good confession before many witnesses.

1 Timothy 6:11–12

. . .

Preach the Good News. Be ready at all times, and tell people what they need to do. Tell them when they are wrong. Encourage them with great patience and careful teaching.

2 Timothy 4:2

52

Ask for help.

Y ou cannot save yourself or conquer your own
sin. But Jesus can, and he waits patiently,
listening for you to call on him. Make your
requests in his name, depending on the merit
and mediation of Christ for God's answer. Ask
with willing submission to the Father's will,
saying in your heart, "Thy will be done." Eagerly
grow dependent on him who can do all things.
Ask for help.

Ask, and God will give to you. Search, and you will find. Knock, and the door will open for you. Yes, everyone who asks will receive. Everyone who searches will find. And everyone who knocks will have the door opened.

MATTHEW 7:7–8

. . .

So I tell you to believe that you have received the things you ask for in prayer, and God will give them to you.

MARK 11:24

. . .

And if you ask for anything in my name, I will do it for you so that the Father's glory will be shown through the Son. If you ask me for anything in my name, I will do it.

JOHN 14:13–14

. . .

But if any of you needs wisdom, you should ask God for it. He is generous to everyone and will give you wisdom without criticizing you.

JAMES 1:5

53

EMBRACE EVERY OPPORTUNITY.

Opportunities are placed in your path every day, not to test your faith and will, but to reveal your faith and will to you. Use every opportunity to share your faith, for the more often you do, the easier it becomes. Let your conduct be thoughtful and wise. Do not provoke criticism, annoyance, and rejection, but say what is relevant and best for each occasion. Embrace every opportunity.

When we have the opportunity to help anyone, we should do it. But we should give special attention to those who are in the family of believers.

GALATIANS 6:10

. . .

So be very careful how you live. Do not live like those who are not wise, but live wisely. Use every chance you have for doing good, because these are evil times. So do not be foolish but learn what the Lord wants you to do.

EPHESIANS 5:15–17

. . .

Be wise in the way you act with people who are not believers, making the most of every opportunity.

COLOSSIANS 4:5

. . .

Are there those among you who are truly wise and understanding? Then they should show it by living right and doing good things with a gentleness that comes from wisdom.

JAMES 3:13

54

Share good news.

Jesus instructed his disciples to go out and make disciples of all nations, and they, in turn, instructed us to share and teach the Scriptures. The Holy Spirit works within you as you share the good news; therefore, have faith and speak publicly, and good words will come from your mouth. Faith in the gospel—nourished in the heart and openly confessed—will secure your salvation. Your belief must be more than a mental exercise; it should bring all your being into a loving trust and willing obedience to Christ. As often as you can, share good news.

Then Jesus came to them and said, "All power in heaven and on earth is given to me. So go and make followers of all people in the world. Baptize them in the name of the Father and the Son and the Holy Spirit."

MATTHEW 28:18–19

· · ·

I will give you the wisdom to say things that none of your enemies will be able to stand against or prove wrong.

LUKE 21:15

· · ·

He told us to preach to the people and to tell them that he is the one whom God chose to be the judge of the living and the dead. All the prophets say it is true that all who believe in Jesus will be forgiven of their sins through Jesus' name.

ACTS 10:42–43

· · ·

Until I come, continue to read the Scriptures to the people, strengthen them, and teach them.

1 TIMOTHY 4:13

55

HONOR YOUR PROMISES.

If you are of Christ, you must be truthful in your words and deeds. Just as you expect God to honor his promises, so should you honor your promises—not only your promises to him but also your promises to others. To willingly lie and betray brings shame to the Lord whom you represent. Honor your promises.

You have heard that it was said to our people long ago, "Don't break your promises, but keep the promises you make to the Lord."

MATTHEW 5:33

. . .

Say only yes if you mean yes, and no if you mean no. If you say more than yes or no, it is from the Evil One.

MATTHEW 5:37

. . .

He never doubted that God would keep his promise, and he never stopped believing. He grew stronger in his faith and gave praise to God.

ROMANS 4:20

. . .

Do not lie to each other. You have left your old sinful life and the things you did before.

COLOSSIANS 3:9

56

Use your gifts.

You cannot do everything, but you can do something. So do something, even if it seems small. Your deed may well be a huge thing to someone else. You are blessed with gifts as you are best able to use them, just as others are blessed with different gifts for different uses. God's gifts to us vary in manner and form, but all should be committed to the service of the Lord. Use your gifts.

And Christ gave gifts to people—he made some to be apostles, some to be prophets, some to go and tell the Good News, and some to have the work of caring for and teaching God's people. Christ gave those gifts to prepare God's holy people for the work of serving, to make the body of Christ stronger.

EPHESIANS 4:11–12

. . .

There are different kinds of gifts, but they are all from the same Spirit. There are different ways to serve but the same Lord to serve. And there are different ways that God works through people but the same God. God works in all of us in everything we do. Something from the Spirit can be seen in each person, for the common good.

1 CORINTHIANS 12:4–7

. . .

It is the same with you. Since you want spiritual gifts very much, seek most of all to have the gifts that help the church grow stronger.

1 CORINTHIANS 14:12

57

TURN FROM DARKNESS.

One cannot both indulge in the deeds of darkness and wear the armor of light. Light represents truth, knowledge, and holiness. Darkness represents ignorance, error, falsehood, and sin. Darkness will cause you to worry about your salvation, paralyze you with guilt, and keep you from being a productive Christian. Dishonesty thrives in the night, but children of the day will walk honestly. An honest, upright, pure life needs no hiding place. Love the Lord, shine, and bring others with you into the light. Turn from darkness.

Your eye is a light for the body. When your eyes are good, your whole body will be full of light. But when your eyes are evil, your whole body will be full of darkness. So be careful not to let the light in you become darkness.

Luke 11:34–35

. . .

I have come as light into the world so that whoever believes in me would not stay in darkness.

John 12:46

. . .

The "night" is almost finished, and the "day" is almost here. So we should stop doing things that belong to darkness and take up the weapons used for fighting in the light.

Romans 13:12

. . .

Have nothing to do with the things done in darkness, which are not worth anything. But show that they are wrong. It is shameful even to talk about what those people do in secret. But the light makes all things easy to see, and everything that is made easy to see can become light.

Ephesians 5:11–14

58

Celebrate every win.

You are an evangelist. Rejoice in the Lord and serve him in your daily battle, for every new believer marks a triumph over darkness. Celebrate the power of the gospel to comfort one who turned away from evil and toward Christ. Thanks be to God for the victory over sin and death through Christ! Celebrate every win!

In the same way, there is joy in the presence of the angels of God when one sinner changes his heart and life.

LUKE 15:10

. . .

In the same way, I tell you there is more joy in heaven over one sinner who changes his heart and life, than over ninety-nine good people who don't need to change.

LUKE 15:7

. . .

We had to celebrate and be happy because your brother was dead, but now he is alive. He was lost, but now he is found.

LUKE 15:32

. . .

When the believers heard this, they stopped arguing. They praised God and said, "So God is allowing even other nations to turn to him and live."

ACTS 11:18

. . .

But we thank God! He gives us the victory through our Lord Jesus Christ.

1 CORINTHIANS 15:57

59

BE NOT BOASTFUL.

Do good deeds simply because good deeds need to be done, not to gain recognition from men or rewards in heaven. It is the deed motivated by grace and humility that pleases God. Take an honest look at your motives and choose to humble yourself before others, for God lifts up the humble. Be not boastful.

So when you give to the poor, don't let anyone know what you are doing. Your giving should be done in secret. Your Father can see what is done in secret, and he will reward you.

MATTHEW 6:3–4

· · ·

Because God has given me a special gift, I have something to say to everyone among you. Do not think you are better than you are. You must decide what you really are by the amount of faith God has given you.

ROMANS 12:3

· · ·

He chose what the world thinks is unimportant and what the world looks down on and thinks is nothing in order to destroy what the world thinks is important. God did this so that no one can brag in his presence.

1 CORINTHIANS 1:28–29

· · ·

"If people want to brag, they should brag only about the Lord." It is not those who say they are good who are accepted but those the Lord thinks are good.

2 CORINTHIANS 10:17–18

60

Repay your debts.

Repay not just your financial debts but your relationship debts and spiritual debts too. One who is rich in Christ cannot deprive a neighbor. Every obligation must be satisfied, every debt paid. Let no debt remain due to anyone except the immortal debt of mutual love, which is due in full to one another, forever and ever. Repay your debts.

Do not owe people anything, except always owe love to each other, because the person who loves others has obeyed all the law.

ROMANS 13:8

. . .

If he has done anything wrong to you or if he owes you anything, charge that to me. I, Paul, am writing this with my own hand. I will pay it back, and I will say nothing about what you owe me for your own life.

PHILEMON VV. 18–19

. . .

The pay you did not give the workers who mowed your fields cries out against you, and the cries of the workers have been heard by the Lord All-Powerful.

JAMES 5:4

61

PUT ASIDE DIFFERENCES.

It is said a house divided against itself cannot stand, and neither can the body of believers. Put aside differences and unite as believers, strengthening each other and the church for the sake of Christ. Avoid rash judgments and a desire to find fault in others. God respects moral character, not appearances, wealth, or earthly rank. Put aside differences.

Each one of us has a body with many parts, and these parts all have different uses. In the same way, we are many, but in Christ we are all one body. Each one is a part of that body, and each part belongs to all the other parts.

ROMANS 12:4–5

. . .

Christ accepted you, so you should accept each other, which will bring glory to God.

ROMANS 15:7

. . .

My dear brothers and sisters, as believers in our glorious Lord Jesus Christ, never think some people are more important than others. Suppose someone comes into your church meeting wearing nice clothes and a gold ring. At the same time a poor person comes in wearing old, dirty clothes. You show special attention to the one wearing nice clothes and say, "Please, sit here in this good seat." But you say to the poor person, "Stand over there," or, "Sit on the floor by my feet." What are you doing? You are making some people more important than others, and with evil thoughts you are deciding that one person is better.

JAMES 2:1–4

62

Answer when asked.

The Lord asks us to tell others about him in order to spread his message to the world. Conduct yourself as though you belong to the Lord, and when asked why you behave as you do, eagerly explain why. Use encouraging words; let Christ be honored and praised in your answer, claiming him as the reason for your hope. Don't be embarrassed or shy; seek to please God instead of men with what you say. Answer when asked.

*I will give you the wisdom to say things that none of your
enemies will be able to stand against or prove wrong.*

LUKE 21:15

. . .

*But during the night, an angel of the Lord opened
the doors of the jail and led the apostles outside.
The angel said, "Go stand in the Temple and tell the
people everything about this new life."*

ACTS 5:19–20

. . .

*When you talk, you should always be kind and
pleasant so you will be able to answer
everyone in the way you should.*

COLOSSIANS 4:6

. . .

*But respect Christ as the holy Lord in your hearts.
Always be ready to answer everyone who asks you
to explain about the hope you have.*

1 PETER 3:15

63

GIVE SECOND CHANCES.

You are not forgiven only once, but each and every time you repent of your sins. Be honest about your imperfections, and you will truly find reason to repent each and every day. And remember, just as you are imperfect, so are those around you. Forgive your neighbors as Jesus forgives you, as often as he forgives you. Give second chances.

Jesus answered, "I tell you, you must forgive him more than seven times. You must forgive him even if he does wrong to you seventy times seven."

MATTHEW 18:22

. . .

When you are praying, if you are angry with someone, forgive him so that your Father in heaven will also forgive your sins.

MARK 11:25

. . .

If he sins against you seven times in one day and says that he is sorry each time, forgive him.

LUKE 17:4

. . .

But now you should forgive him and comfort him to keep him from having too much sadness and giving up completely.

2 CORINTHIANS 2:7

. . .

Since he himself is weak, he is able to be gentle with those who do not understand and who are doing wrong things.

HEBREWS 5:2

64

Turn from excess.

Excess of any kind will lead you astray; turn away from it and toward the will of God. You are to rid yourself of your former way of life and put on a new self, one created to be like God in true righteousness and holiness. Do not live the rest of your life for unholy desires, but rather for the will of God. If you are guided by the Spirit, you will not obey the lusts of the flesh and temptations of evil. Act like Jesus, and find yourself satisfied in higher and eternal ways. Turn from excess.

Let us live in a right way, like people who belong to the day. We should not have wild parties or get drunk. There should be no sexual sins of any kind, no fighting or jealousy.

Romans 13:13

. . .

So I tell you: Live by following the Spirit. Then you will not do what your sinful selves want. Our sinful selves want what is against the Spirit, and the Spirit wants what is against our sinful selves. The two are against each other, so you cannot do just what you please.

Galatians 5:16–17

. . .

You were taught to leave your old self—to stop living the evil way you lived before. That old self becomes worse, because people are fooled by the evil things they want to do. But you were taught to be made new in your hearts, to become a new person. That new person is made to be like God—made to be truly good and holy.

Ephesians 4:22–24

65

KNOW YOUR PURPOSE.

The gospel is not for a few favored ones, but for everyone. Realize that your purpose is not *your* purpose, but *his* purpose. Give yourself fully to him; labor for the Lord, making him known through your words and deeds. Know—and fulfill—your purpose.

We know that in everything God works for the good of those who love him. They are the people he called, because that was his plan.

ROMANS 8:28

. . .

And there are different ways that God works through people but the same God. God works in all of us in everything we do.

1 CORINTHIANS 12:6

. . .

So my dear brothers and sisters, stand strong. Do not let anything move you. Always give yourselves fully to the work of the Lord, because you know that your work in the Lord is never wasted.

1 CORINTHIANS 15:58

. . .

So we continue to preach Christ to each person, using all wisdom to warn and to teach everyone, in order to bring each one into God's presence as a mature person in Christ.

COLOSSIANS 1:28

66

Pause to reflect.

Knowledge and wisdom are the products of reflection. Pause, reflect, consider what the Lord has done for you, and become wise in the ways he would have you to live. Examine your thoughts, words, and deeds, and take the necessary steps to align yourself in proper relationship with Christ. Do not compare yourself to what others do, but instead strive to please God in all that you do. Do this and you will know the Lord. Pause to reflect.

Look closely at yourselves. Test yourselves to see if you are living in the faith. You know that Jesus Christ is in you—unless you fail the test.

2 Corinthians 13:5

. . .

If anyone thinks he is important when he really is not, he is only fooling himself. Each person should judge his own actions and not compare himself with others. Then he can be proud for what he himself has done.

Galatians 6:3–4

. . .

Brothers and sisters, think about the things that are good and worthy of praise. Think about the things that are true and honorable and right and pure and beautiful and respected.

Philippians 4:8

. . .

Think about what I am saying, because the Lord will give you the ability to understand everything.

2 Timothy 2:7

67

DENY SELFISH PLEASURES.

Self-indulgence disgraces the Lord, for it was his self-sacrifice that gave you the promise of life. A lack of restraint also discourages other Christians who may be weak in their faith and looking to you as an encourager. Pursue what is right, and acknowledge Christ with your unselfish conduct. If you know how to do the right thing and choose not to, your sin is greater because of your knowledge. But if you conquer temptation and give yourself entirely to God, he will work mightily in you. Deny selfish pleasures.

[Moses] chose to suffer with God's people instead of enjoying sin for a short time. He thought it was better to suffer for the Christ than to have all the treasures of Egypt, because he was looking for God's reward.

HEBREWS 11:25–26

. . .

In the past we also were foolish. We did not obey, we were wrong, and we were slaves to many things our bodies wanted and enjoyed. We spent our lives doing evil and being jealous. People hated us, and we hated each other. But when the kindness and love of God our Savior was shown, he saved us because of his mercy. It was not because of good deeds we did to be right with him. He saved us through the washing that made us new people through the Holy Spirit.

TITUS 3:3–5

. . .

You want things, but you do not have them. So you are ready to kill and are jealous of other people, but you still cannot get what you want. So you argue and fight. You do not get what you want, because you do not ask God. Or when you ask, you do not receive because the reason you ask is wrong. You want things so you can use them for your own pleasures.

JAMES 4:2–3

68

ACT WITH PATIENCE.

Do nothing that would discourage others from turning to Christ, but instead let the Holy Spirit use you to inspire others to follow Christ. If your heart is filled with love, patience will be one of your defining qualities and a reason why others draw nearer to you. Patience leaves time for anger to fade away. Act with patience.

Always be humble, gentle, and patient,
accepting each other in love.

Ephesians 4:2

. . .

But I was given mercy so that in me, the worst of all
sinners, Christ Jesus could show that he has patience
without limit. His patience with me made me an example
for those who would believe in him and have life forever.

1 Timothy 1:16

. . .

Preach the Good News. Be ready at all times, and
tell people what they need to do. Tell them when
they are wrong. Encourage them with great
patience and careful teaching.

2 Timothy 4:2

. . .

Brothers and sisters, be patient until the Lord comes
again. A farmer patiently waits for his valuable crop to
grow from the earth and for it to receive the autumn
and spring rains. You, too, must be patient. Do not
give up hope, because the Lord is coming soon.

James 5:7–8

69

STRIVE FOR HARMONY.

In harmony with one another we share the love of Christ and become examples of the goodness accomplished in his name. But in conflict with one another we work against his purpose and distract everyone from the gospel. Live together in peace, spreading goodwill among men. Strive for harmony.

Keep on loving each other as brothers and sisters.

HEBREWS 13:1

. . .

*People who work for peace in a peaceful way
plant a good crop of right-living.*

JAMES 3:18

. . .

*Finally, all of you should be in agreement,
understanding each other, loving each other
as family, being kind and humble.*

1 PETER 3:8

. . .

*They are blessed who show mercy to others, for God will
show mercy to them. They are blessed whose thoughts
are pure, for they will see God. They are blessed who
work for peace, for they will be called God's children.*

MATTHEW 5:7–9

70

Overcome your worry.

God gave you life, and he will see that it is nourished if you trust in him. If you turn away from worldly troubles, seek the kingdom, and call on the Lord, all things needed will be given to you. Do your duty, fully trusting that God will see that you do not go without necessary things. Instead of worry, lay your case before God, not as a complaint but with thanks for his mercy, and you will find the peace that comes after putting all in the hands of the One who is able and willing to help you. Overcome your worry.

Jesus said to his followers, "So I tell you, don't worry about the food you need to live, or about the clothes you need for your body. Life is more than food, and the body is more than clothes. Look at the birds. They don't plant or harvest, they don't have storerooms or barns, but God feeds them. And you are worth much more than birds."

LUKE 12:22–24

. . .

I leave you peace; my peace I give you. I do not give it to you as the world does. So don't let your hearts be troubled or afraid.

JOHN 14:27

. . .

Do not worry about anything, but pray and ask God for everything you need, always giving thanks. And God's peace, which is so great we cannot understand it, will keep your hearts and minds in Christ Jesus.

PHILIPPIANS 4:6–7

. . .

Humble yourselves, therefore, under God's mighty hand, that he may lift you up in due time. Cast all your anxiety on him because he cares for you.

1 PETER 5:6–7 NIV

71

PATIENTLY ENDURE TESTING.

The Lord is full of compassion and mercy, but he works in his own time. Resist impatience, stand firm in your conviction, and remain confident as you wait. Faith that endures earns the crown. Remember God's promise: he will not burden you with more than you can bear. Under God's plan, all things—even your sorrow, trials, and persecutions—work together for your blessing (Romans 8:28). Patiently endure testing.

God will strengthen you with his own great power so that you will not give up when troubles come, but you will be patient.

COLOSSIANS 1:11

. . .

So we do not give up. Our physical body is becoming older and weaker, but our spirit inside us is made new every day. We have small troubles for a while now, but they are helping us gain an eternal glory that is much greater than the troubles.

2 CORINTHIANS 4:16–17

. . .

When people are tempted and still continue strong, they should be happy. After they have proved their faith, God will reward them with life forever. God promised this to all those who love him.

JAMES 1:12

. . .

Control yourselves and be careful! The devil, your enemy, goes around like a roaring lion looking for someone to eat. Refuse to give in to him, by standing strong in your faith. You know that your Christian family all over the world is having the same kinds of suffering.

1 PETER 5:8–9

72

Remember your renewal.

In Christ you are renewed; by his grace you were restored. Realize your dependence on him and your complete inability to restore yourself. All who come to Christ escape from sin and corruption, but sometimes your old ways resurface and tempt you into sin. When this happens, repent at once and flee to Christ! Do not forget your cleansing. Honor and proclaim the work that Christ has performed in and for you. Remember your renewal.

*Do not conform any longer to the pattern of this world,
but be transformed by the renewing of your mind.
Then you will be able to test and approve what God's
will is—his good, pleasing and perfect will.*

<small>ROMANS 12:2 NIV</small>

. . .

*If all these things are in you and are growing, they will
help you to be useful and productive in your knowledge of
our Lord Jesus Christ. But anyone who does not have
these things cannot see clearly. He is blind and has
forgotten that he was made clean from his past sins.*

<small>2 PETER 1:8–9</small>

. . .

*Christ gave you a special gift that is still in you, so
you do not need any other teacher. His gift teaches
you about everything, and it is true, not false. So
continue to live in Christ, as his gift taught you.*

<small>1 JOHN 2:27</small>

. . .

*Those who are God's children do not continue sinning, because
the new life from God remains in them. They are not able to go
on sinning, because they have become children of God.*

<small>1 JOHN 3:9</small>

73

FORGET THE PAST.

Your old self, the one from your past and before the time of your renewal, was corrupted by your imperfect judgment and unjust desires. Now your new self, guided by righteous obedience, should turn away from all your former sins. Look ahead, always seeking God's will, never returning to the old ways that separated you from your salvation. Forget the past.

You were taught to leave your old self—to stop living the evil way you lived before. That old self becomes worse, because people are fooled by the evil things they want to do. But you were taught to be made new in your hearts, to become a new person. That new person is made to be like God—made to be truly good and holy.

EPHESIANS 4:22–24

. . .

Now that you are obedient children of God do not live as you did in the past. You did not understand, so you did the evil things you wanted.

1 PETER 1:14

. . .

You know that in the past you were living in a worthless way, a way passed down from the people who lived before you. But you were saved from that useless life. You were bought, not with something that ruins like gold or silver, but with the precious blood of Christ, who was like a pure and perfect lamb.

1 PETER 1:18–19

74

Envision your future.

What lies ahead for believers is far greater than anything that has or will come to pass in the present world. This is the promise of God: eternal life with a heavenly inheritance rich beyond your conception. Pray for his kingdom to come! Envision your future.

If we are God's children, we will receive blessings from God together with Christ. But we must suffer as Christ suffered so that we will have glory as Christ has glory. The sufferings we have now are nothing compared to the great glory that will be shown to us.

Romans 8:17–18

. . .

Do not be lazy but work hard, serving the Lord with all your heart. Be joyful because you have hope. Be patient when trouble comes, and pray at all times.

Romans 12:11–12

. . .

Training your body helps you in some ways, but serving God helps you in every way by bringing you blessings in this life and in the future life, too. What I say is true, and you should fully accept it. This is why we work and struggle: We hope in the living God who is the Savior of all people, especially of those who believe.

1 Timothy 4:8–10

75

FOCUS YOUR GOAL.

You have but one goal: to please the Lord. Spend your time and energy in constant devotion to him, giving your whole life to his praise and glory, pressing through every difficulty in your faithful pursuit of that goal, and you will prosper with heavenly treasures. To labor only for worldly treasures is to labor in vain. Focus your goal.

So my dear brothers and sisters, stand strong. Do not let anything move you. Always give yourselves fully to the work of the Lord, because you know that your work in the Lord is never wasted.

1 CORINTHIANS 15:58

. . .

We live by what we believe, not by what we can see. So I say that we have courage. We really want to be away from this body and be at home with the Lord. Our only goal is to please God whether we live here or there.

2 CORINTHIANS 5:7–9

. . .

I do not mean that I am already as God wants me to be. I have not yet reached that goal, but I continue trying to reach it and to make it mine. Christ wants me to do that, which is the reason he made me his. Brothers and sisters, I know that I have not yet reached that goal, but there is one thing I always do. Forgetting the past and straining toward what is ahead, I keep trying to reach the goal and get the prize for which God called me through Christ to the life above.

PHILIPPIANS 3:12–14

76

DO YOUR SHARE.

Do as much as you can in line with your blessings and abilities, no matter how high or low the task may be. You can do your part with joy, knowing you are a model of Christ's great love and mercy. This pleases the Lord. Do your share.

You know I always worked to take care of my own needs and the needs of those who were with me.

Acts 20:34

. . .

Brothers and sisters, by the authority of our Lord Jesus Christ we command you to stay away from any believer who refuses to work and does not follow the teaching we gave you. You yourselves know that you should live as we live. We were not lazy when we were with you. And when we ate another person's food, we always paid for it. We worked very hard night and day so we would not be an expense to any of you. We had the right to ask you to help us, but we worked to take care of ourselves so we would be an example for you to follow.

2 Thessalonians 3:6–9

. . .

We want each of you to go on with the same hard work all your lives so you will surely get what you hope for. We do not want you to become lazy. Be like those who through faith and patience will receive what God has promised.

Hebrews 6:11–12

77

COMFORT YOUR BROTHER.

Christ, the perfect one without sin, laid down his life for us, the sinners. In return, he asked that we give comfort to those in trouble, sharing the comfort that we first received from him. If you love as he loved, you cannot refuse to comfort your suffering brother. Let your love be deep and enduring, not shallow and brief. Comfort your brother.

He comforts us every time we have trouble, so when others have trouble, we can comfort them with the same comfort God gives us.

2 CORINTHIANS 1:4

. . .

I have great joy and comfort, my brother, because the love you have shown to God's people has refreshed them.

PHILEMON v. 7

. . .

Remember those who are in prison as if you were in prison with them. Remember those who are suffering as if you were suffering with them.

HEBREWS 13:3

. . .

This is how we know what love is: Jesus Christ laid down his life for us. And we ought to lay down our lives for our brothers. If anyone has material possessions and sees his brother in need but has no pity on him, how can the love of God be in him? Dear children, let us not love with words or tongue but with actions and in truth. This then is how we know that we belong to the truth, and how we set our hearts at rest in his presence.

1 JOHN 3:16–19 NIV

78

Parent with love.

Unreasonable scolding, hurtful language, or cruel punishment brings about resentment in children, making you ineffective in the Christian training of your children. Love them as Jesus loved them—with patience, kindness, protection, trust, and hope, always keeping them from becoming discouraged. This is the way in which your Lord loves you; follow his example. Parent with love.

Then Jesus took the children in his arms, put his hands on them, and blessed them.

MARK 10:16

. . .

Love is patient and kind. Love is not jealous, it does not brag, and it is not proud. Love is not rude, is not selfish, and does not get upset with others. Love does not count up wrongs that have been done. Love takes no pleasure in evil but rejoices over the truth. Love patiently accepts all things. It always trusts, always hopes, and always endures.

1 CORINTHIANS 13:4–7

. . .

Fathers, do not make your children angry, but raise them with the training and teaching of the Lord.

EPHESIANS 6:4

. . .

Fathers, do not nag your children. If you are too hard to please, they may want to stop trying.

COLOSSIANS 3:21

79

LOVE WITHOUT HESITATION.

You cannot profess to follow Christ unless you love all those for whom Christ died. We were instructed to love our neighbor as we love ourselves. Love each other so well that there will be kindness and mutual acts of service between you. All relationships are made perfect if filled with love but are worthless without it. Love without hesitation.

I give you a new command: Love each other. You must love each other as I have loved you.

JOHN 13:34

. . .

Do not owe people anything, except always owe love to each other, because the person who loves others has obeyed all the law.

ROMANS 13:8

. . .

I may have the gift of prophecy. I may understand all the secret things of God and have all knowledge, and I may have faith so great I can move mountains. But even with all these things, if I do not have love, then I am nothing. I may give away everything I have, and I may even give my body as an offering to be burned. But I gain nothing if I do not have love.

1 CORINTHIANS 13:2–3

. . .

Now that your obedience to the truth has purified your souls, you can have true love for your Christian brothers and sisters. So love each other deeply with all your heart.

1 PETER 1:22

80

Choose good company.

Bad company corrupts good character, period. Do not be led astray by unbelievers who mock your faith. Turn to the body of believers for your spiritual companionship and fortification, and bask in the fellowship of that safe harbor, for the church and its members are a well-provisioned refuge from the temptations of darkness. Choose good company.

Brothers and sisters, I ask you to look out for those who cause people to be against each other and who upset other people's faith. They are against the true teaching you learned, so stay away from them.

Romans 16:17

. . .

Do not be fooled: "Bad friends will ruin good habits."

1 Corinthians 15:33

. . .

So, you are not loyal to God! You should know that loving the world is the same as hating God. Anyone who wants to be a friend of the world becomes God's enemy.

James 4:4

. . .

My dear friend, do not follow what is bad; follow what is good. The one who does good belongs to God. But the one who does evil has never known God.

3 John v. 11

81

SHARE YOURSELF WILLINGLY.

Remember, there are no greater gifts to share than your time, labor, and love. Whoever sows sparingly of these will also reap sparingly, and whoever sows generously will also reap generously. Do not forget to give yourself away, for with such sacrifices God is well pleased. Share yourself willingly.

Remember this: The person who plants a little will have a small harvest, but the person who plants a lot will have a big harvest.

2 Corinthians 9:6

. . .

We loved you so much that we were delighted to share with you not only the gospel of God but our lives as well, because you had become so dear to us.

1 Thessalonians 2:8 niv

. . .

So through Jesus let us always offer to God our sacrifice of praise, coming from lips that speak his name. Do not forget to do good to others, and share with them, because such sacrifices please God.

Hebrews 13:15–16

. . .

Open your homes to each other, without complaining.

1 Peter 4:9

82

Hold yourself accountable.

Although saved, we remain imperfect people who continue to be tempted by our sinful nature. Do not take salvation for granted and act as though you are unchanged. Train yourself to be godly, obey the Word, and rise above your nature, demonstrating your renewal so that others may wish to follow your example. Obedience to God is the sign of your sheer delight and a joy-filled thankfulness for your salvation. Hold yourself accountable.

Stay awake and pray for strength against temptation. The spirit wants to do what is right, but the body is weak.

MATTHEW 26:41

. . .

Brothers, if someone is caught in a sin, you who are spiritual should restore him gently. But watch yourself, or you also may be tempted.

GALATIANS 6:1 NIV

. . .

But do not follow foolish stories that disagree with God's truth, but train yourself to serve God.

1 TIMOTHY 4:7

. . .

Share in the troubles we have like a good soldier of Christ Jesus. A soldier wants to please the enlisting officer, so no one serving in the army wastes time with everyday matters. Also an athlete who takes part in a contest must obey all the rules in order to win.

2 TIMOTHY 2:3–5

83

PROTECT THE WEAK.

In everything you do, help those who are weak in strength, self-control, and faith. Bear with their shortcomings, do not exploit them, and remember Jesus' compassion for those unable to help themselves except by their dependence on him. Protect the weak.

I showed you in all things that you should work as I did and help the weak. I taught you to remember the words Jesus said: "It is more blessed to give than to receive."

ACTS 20:35

. . .

We who are strong in faith should help the weak with their weaknesses, and not please only ourselves.

ROMANS 15:1

. . .

But be careful that your freedom does not cause those who are weak in faith to fall into sin.

1 CORINTHIANS 8:9

. . .

We ask you, brothers and sisters, to warn those who do not work. Encourage the people who are afraid. Help those who are weak. Be patient with everyone.

1 THESSALONIANS 5:14

84

Make a difference.

Jesus told us to use our earthly resources to gain
friends by making a real difference in their lives,
and to then lead them to him. Therefore, do not
hold on tightly to what you have been blessed with,
but apportion it for the greater good. The faithful
steward will be trusted with more. Make a
difference.

Give, and you will receive. You will be given much. Pressed down, shaken together, and running over, it will spill into your lap. The way you give to others is the way God will give to you.

Luke 6:38

. . .

Each one should give as you have decided in your heart to give. You should not be sad when you give, and you should not give because you feel forced to give. God loves the person who gives happily.

2 Corinthians 9:7

. . .

The only thing they asked us was to remember to help the poor—something I really wanted to do.

Galatians 2:10

. . .

Do not forget to do good to others, and share with them, because such sacrifices please God.

Hebrews 13:16

85

BELIEVE IN MIRACLES.

Miracles are the evidence of God's existence, shown to you so that you might more easily believe in him. However, those who believe without seeing are even more blessed, for they walk by faith instead of sight. Grow your faith and you will grow more intimate with the Lord. Even if you've never seen one, believe in miracles.

Jesus went everywhere in Galilee, teaching in the synagogues, preaching the Good News about the kingdom of heaven, and healing all the people's diseases and sicknesses. The news about Jesus spread all over Syria, and people brought all the sick to him. They were suffering from different kinds of diseases. Some were in great pain, some had demons, some were epileptics, and some were paralyzed. Jesus healed all of them.

MATTHEW 4:23–24

. . .

So in Cana of Galilee Jesus did his first miracle. There he showed his glory, and his followers believed in him.

JOHN 2:11

. . .

Believe me when I say that I am in the Father and the Father is in me. Or believe because of the miracles I have done.

JOHN 14:11

. . .

God also testified to the truth of the message by using wonders, great signs, many kinds of miracles, and by giving people gifts through the Holy Spirit, just as he wanted.

HEBREWS 2:4

86

Accept what comes.

Even if you should suffer for doing or saying what is right, you are blessed. If it is God's will, a harvest of righteousness and peace is your reward for not becoming weary of what is right. Evil will try to undo good works, but boldly facing evil strengthens what is good. Do not surrender; but rather, be strengthened by your faith. Accept what comes.

Jesus looked at his followers and said, "You people who are poor are blessed, because the kingdom of God belongs to you. You people who are now hungry are blessed, because you will be satisfied. You people who are now crying are blessed, because you will laugh with joy. People will hate you, shut you out, insult you, and say you are evil because you follow the Son of Man. But when they do, you will be blessed."

LUKE 6:20–22

· · ·

We must not become tired of doing good. We will receive our harvest of eternal life at the right time if we do not give up.

GALATIANS 6:9

· · ·

A person might have to suffer even when it is unfair, but if he thinks of God and can stand the pain, God is pleased.

1 PETER 2:19

· · ·

If you are trying hard to do good, no one can really hurt you. But even if you suffer for doing right, you are blessed. "Don't be afraid of what they fear; do not dread those things." But respect Christ as the holy Lord in your hearts.

1 PETER 3:13–15

87

CONQUER YOUR WILL.

This is the confidence you have in approaching God: that if you ask for anything according to his will, he hears you. Submit yourself, then, to God. Come near to him, and he will come near to you. Do not be foolish, but understand what the Lord's will is: that you turn away from your own will, which, being of the flesh, always leads you astray. Conquer your will.

Jesus answered, "If people love me, they will obey my teaching. My Father will love them, and we will come to them and make our home with them."

JOHN 14:23

. . .

The world and its desires pass away, but the man who does the will of God lives forever.

1 JOHN 2:17 NIV

. . .

And this is the boldness we have in God's presence: that if we ask God for anything that agrees with what he wants, he hears us.

1 JOHN 5:14

. . .

So give yourselves completely to God. Stand against the devil, and the devil will run from you. Come near to God, and God will come near to you. You sinners, clean sin out of your lives. You who are trying to follow God and the world at the same time, make your thinking pure.

JAMES 4:7–8

88

Yield to wisdom.

The foolishness of God is wiser than your wisdom, and the weakness of God is stronger than your strength. If you rely on your own wisdom in all things, you fail to seek the will of God. If you seek the will of God, you will have divine wisdom in your thinking and peace in your heart. In all matters, ask Christ to go with you and bless you in what you are about to undertake. Yield to *his* wisdom.

*Even the foolishness of God is wiser than
human wisdom, and the weakness of God
is stronger than human strength.*

1 Corinthians 1:25

. . .

*And we speak about these things, not with words
taught us by human wisdom but with words
taught us by the Spirit. And so we explain
spiritual truths to spiritual people.*

1 Corinthians 2:13

. . .

*Obey your leaders and act under their authority.
They are watching over you, because they are
responsible for your souls. Obey them so that they
will do this work with joy, not sadness. It will not
help you to make their work hard.*

Hebrews 13:17

. . .

*But if any of you needs wisdom, you should ask
God for it. He is generous to everyone and will
give you wisdom without criticizing you.*

James 1:5

89

LIVE IN TODAY.

Do not rest on what you have done in the past or bank on what you plan to do in the future, for yesterday is gone and tomorrow may never come. Live as if it were your last day, surrendering every aspect of your life to God, seeking to live more and more as Christ lived, even in your final moments. Don't wait for tomorrow. Live in today.

Don't worry and say, "What will we eat?" or "What will we drink?" or "What will we wear?" The people who don't know God keep trying to get these things, and your Father in heaven knows you need them. Seek first God's kingdom and what God wants. Then all your other needs will be met as well. So don't worry about tomorrow, because tomorrow will have its own worries. Each day has enough trouble of its own.

MATTHEW 6:31–34

. . .

God says, "At the right time I heard your prayers. On the day of salvation I helped you." I tell you that the "right time" is now, and the "day of salvation" is now.

2 CORINTHIANS 6:2

. . .

Some of you say, "Today or tomorrow we will go to some city. We will stay there a year, do business, and make money." But you do not know what will happen tomorrow! Your life is like a mist. You can see it for a short time, but then it goes away. So you should say, "If the Lord wants, we will live and do this or that."

JAMES 4:13–15

90

Believe in tomorrow.

If the day of the Lord seems delayed, it is not due to his idleness. Rather, it is because God is longsuffering and is giving time to all his people to come to repentance. God is not unjust; he will not forget your work and the love you have shown him as you have helped your neighbors and continue to help them. Continue your work of love, and show an equal effort in attaining the full assurance of hope found in Christ. By God's promise, those who believe in his Son will see a new heaven and a new earth. Do more than believe *in* God, *believe* God. Believe in tomorrow.

Remember, God is the One who makes you and us strong in Christ. God made us his chosen people. He put his mark on us to show that we are his, and he put his Spirit in our hearts to be a guarantee for all he has promised.

2 Corinthians 1:21–22

. . .

When you heard the true teaching—the Good News about your salvation—you believed in Christ. And in Christ, God put his special mark of ownership on you by giving you the Holy Spirit that he had promised. That Holy Spirit is the guarantee that we will receive what God promised for his people until God gives full freedom to those who are his—to bring praise to God's glory.

Ephesians 1:13–14

. . .

The Lord is not slow in doing what he promised—the way some people understand slowness. But God is being patient with you. He does not want anyone to be lost, but he wants all people to change their hearts and lives.

2 Peter 3:9

. . .

But God made a promise to us, and we are waiting for a new heaven and a new earth where goodness lives.

2 Peter 3:13

91

ALWAYS HAVE HOPE.

The hope you have in Christ is the source of your greatest joy. Through the sufferings of Christ, you are enabled to come to God; without Christ and his death on the cross, there could be no gospel. As God's child you have a glorious hope of eternal life, a hope not only of eternal existence, but also of becoming a joint heir with Christ. You are reconciled with God when you believe in his Son, grow in your faith, and are not swayed from the truth of the gospel—those who believe in what they cannot see shall inherit an everlasting life. Always have hope.

And we are happy because of the hope we have of sharing God's glory. We also have joy with our troubles, because we know that these troubles produce patience. And patience produces character, and character produces hope. And this hope will never disappoint us, because God has poured out his love to fill our hearts. He gave us his love through the Holy Spirit, whom God has given to us.

ROMANS 5:2–5

. . .

I pray that the God who gives hope will fill you with much joy and peace while you trust in him. Then your hope will overflow by the power of the Holy Spirit.

ROMANS 15:13

. . .

Praise be to the God and Father of our Lord Jesus Christ. In God's great mercy he has caused us to be born again into a living hope, because Jesus Christ rose from the dead. Now we hope for the blessings God has for his children. These blessings, which cannot be destroyed or be spoiled or lose their beauty, are kept in heaven for you.

1 PETER 1:3–4

92

PRAY FOR OTHERS.

Love will repay cursing with blessing, hate with goodwill, evil treatment and persecution with prayers. While on the cross, Jesus prayed for his enemies; he was clear about his desire and his command that we too should pray for others. What greater display of love for your neighbor and brother is there than to bow and pray for him? Please the Lord—pray for others.

I thank my God every time I remember you,
always praying with joy for all of you.

PHILIPPIANS 1:3–4

. . .

Brothers and sisters, pray for us.

1 THESSALONIANS 5:25

. . .

But I say to you who are listening, love your enemies.
Do good to those who hate you, bless those who curse
you, pray for those who are cruel to you.

LUKE 6:27–28

. . .

I always remember you in my prayers, asking the
God of our Lord Jesus Christ, the glorious Father, to
give you a spirit of wisdom and revelation so that
you will know him better. I pray also that you will
have greater understanding in your heart so you will
know the hope to which he has called us and that
you will know how rich and glorious are the
blessings God has promised his holy people.

EPHESIANS 1:16–18

93

JUST BE YOURSELF.

Do your best to present yourself to God as one who surely knows and confidently walks like his Son, Jesus Christ. As a believer, think of yourself with sober judgment, with a spirit of power, of love, and of self-discipline, as one unafraid to endure the laughter and scoffs of the nonbeliever. In your resolve, the Word of God and work of Jesus will be made known. With all moral courage, which is the natural fruit of a trusting faith in God, you are one saved by grace. Just be yourself.

*So I strive always to keep my conscience
clear before God and man.*

Acts 24:16 niv

. . .

*Because God has given me a special gift, I have
something to say to everyone among you. Do not think
you are better than you are. You must decide what you
really are by the amount of faith God has given you.*

Romans 12:3

. . .

*So stand strong, with the belt of truth tied around your
waist and the protection of right living on your chest.*

Ephesians 6:14

. . .

*God did not give us a spirit that makes us afraid but
a spirit of power and love and self-control.*

2 Timothy 1:7

. . .

*Make every effort to give yourself to God as the kind of
person he will approve. Be a worker who is not ashamed
and who uses the true teaching in the right way.*

2 Timothy 2:15

94

Make private time.

When you are alone with God, you are free from distraction and the temptation to impress with your actions and words. There are times for public and corporate prayer, and there are times for private prayer. Kneel and be sincere with your Lord. Make private time.

When you pray, don't be like the hypocrites. They love to stand in the synagogues and on the street corners and pray so people will see them. I tell you the truth, they already have their full reward. When you pray, you should go into your room and close the door and pray to your Father who cannot be seen. Your Father can see what is done in secret, and he will reward you.

MATTHEW 6:5–6

• • •

After he had sent them away, he went by himself up into the hills to pray. It was late, and Jesus was there alone.

MATTHEW 14:23

• • •

Then Jesus went with his followers to a place called Gethsemane. He said to them, "Sit here while I go over there and pray."

MATTHEW 26:36

• • •

Early the next morning, while it was still dark, Jesus woke and left the house. He went to a lonely place, where he prayed.

MARK 1:35

95

REST IN ASSURANCE.

We live by faith, not by sight (2 Corinthians 5:7). Faith in Christ pleases God. Instead of many works, only one work is required—a faith that would enable you to rely on Christ and from such faith to lead a Christlike life. God promised to be with you, and his Son died to make that possible. He who has called you is faithful, and if you trust him, he will save you. Your faith will remind you to whom you truly belong. In Jesus Christ, go boldly to God. Rest in assurance.

The world and everything that people want in it are passing away, but the person who does what God wants lives forever.

1 John 2:17

. . .

Yes, I am sure that neither death, nor life, nor angels, nor ruling spirits, nothing now, nothing in the future, no powers, nothing above us, nothing below us, nor anything else in the whole world will ever be able to separate us from the love of God that is in Christ Jesus our Lord.

Romans 8:38–39

. . .

In Christ we can come before God with freedom and without fear. We can do this through faith in Christ.

Ephesians 3:12

. . .

Now may God himself, the God of peace, make you pure, belonging only to him. May your whole self— spirit, soul, and body—be kept safe and without fault when our Lord Jesus Christ comes. You can trust the One who calls you to do that for you.

1 Thessalonians 5:23–24

96

Study the Word.

The purpose of the Scriptures is to inspire blessed hope through the promise and comfort they offer to those who suffer for God. Everything that was written was written to teach you so that through the encouragement of the Scriptures you might become fully equipped, able to teach the gospel to others and to discourage its opposers. Read your Bible and discover what righteous living really is. The stronger your conviction becomes of what is right, the easier it becomes for you to live righteously. Study the Word.

Jesus answered, "You don't understand, because you don't know what the Scriptures say, and you don't know about the power of God."

. . .

For everything that was written in the past was written to teach us, so that through endurance and the encouragement of the Scriptures we might have hope.

. . .

Until I come, continue to read the Scriptures to the people, strengthen them, and teach them.

1 T IMOTHY 4:13

. . .

All Scripture is given by God and is useful for teaching, for showing people what is wrong in their lives, for correcting faults, and for teaching how to live right.

2 T IMOTHY 3:16

{ 97 }

STRENGTHEN YOUR FOUNDATION.

Do more than just read the Bible; do what it says. Make every effort to add to your faith, goodness; and to goodness, knowledge; and to knowledge, self-control; and to self-control, patience; and to patience, service for God; and to service for God, kindness to your brothers and sisters in Christ; and to your kindness, love (2 Peter 1:5–7). If you seek these qualities in increasing measure, they will keep you from being ineffective and unproductive in your knowledge of your Lord Jesus Christ. Be an effective and productive child of God, refusing to let anyone lead you astray. Strengthen your foundation.

We live by what we believe, not by what we can see.

2 Corinthians 5:7

. . .

Do what God's teaching says; when you only listen and do nothing, you are fooling yourselves.

James 1:22

. . .

Jesus has the power of God, by which he has given us everything we need to live and to serve God. We have these things because we know him. Jesus called us by his glory and goodness. Through these he gave us the very great and precious promises. With these gifts you can share in God's nature, and the world will not ruin you with its evil desires.

2 Peter 1:3–4

. . .

But dear friends, use your most holy faith to build yourselves up, praying in the Holy Spirit. Keep yourselves in God's love as you wait for the Lord Jesus Christ with his mercy to give you life forever.

Jude vv. 20–21

98

Pray every day.

Pray continually, on all occasions with all kinds of prayers, thanksgiving, and requests, for the Lord is faithful (Philippians 4:6). As you draw nearer to him, he will strengthen and protect you, growing you in righteousness and enriching you with blessings. Daily prayer strengthens your walk with Christ, increasing your endurance for his sake. Pray every day.

*Pray in the Spirit at all times with all kinds of
prayers, asking for everything you need. To do this
you must always be ready and never give up.
Always pray for all God's people.*

EPHESIANS 6:18

. . .

*Continue praying, keeping alert,
and always thanking God.*

COLOSSIANS 4:2

. . .

*Always be joyful. Pray continually, and give
thanks whatever happens. That is what
God wants for you in Christ Jesus.*

1 THESSALONIANS 5:16–18

. . .

*So, I want the men everywhere to pray, lifting up their
hands in a holy manner, without anger and arguments.*

1 TIMOTHY 2:8

99

Never give up.

God hears your prayers and pleas but answers in his own time. Jesus encouraged us to always pray and never give up. There must be constant seeking and patient endurance. He who remains faithful shall enter the kingdom. Do not throw away your confidence; hold yourself up in prayer instead. In time, when you have resisted the world and done the will of God, you will be richly rewarded. Never give up.

Some people, by always continuing to do good, live for God's glory, for honor, and for life that has no end. God will give them life forever.

ROMANS 2:7

· · ·

When people are tempted and still continue strong, they should be happy. After they have proved their faith, God will reward them with life forever. God promised this to all those who love him.

JAMES 1:12

· · ·

They said to you, "In the last times there will be people who laugh about God, following their own evil desires which are against God." These are the people who divide you, people whose thoughts are only of this world, who do not have the Spirit. But dear friends, use your most holy faith to build yourselves up, praying in the Holy Spirit. Keep yourselves in God's love as you wait for the Lord Jesus Christ with his mercy to give you life forever.

JUDE VV. 18–21

100

Love the Lord.

After all, he, the manifestation of God in the flesh, loved you first. And when you love him in return and walk faithfully with him, obeying from the heart all his commandments, good things do indeed come to you. Love God, your Father, your Christ, with all your heart, all your soul, all your mind, and all your strength (Mark 12:30). *Love* the Lord. Love *the* Lord. Love the *Lord*.

Love the Lord your God with all your heart, all your soul, all your mind, and all your strength.

MARK 12:30

. . .

You should produce much fruit and show that you are my followers, which brings glory to my Father. I loved you as the Father loved me. Now remain in my love. I have obeyed my Father's commands, and I remain in his love. In the same way, if you obey my commands, you will remain in my love. I have told you these things so that you can have the same joy I have and so that your joy will be the fullest possible joy.

JOHN 15:8–11

. . .

We know that in everything God works for the good of those who love him. They are the people he called, because that was his plan.

ROMANS 8:28

. . .

Every good action and every perfect gift is from God. These good gifts come down from the Creator of the sun, moon, and stars, who does not change like their shifting shadows. God decided to give us life through the word of truth so we might be the most important of all the things he made.

JAMES 1:17–18

ACKNOWLEDGMENTS

Some of those who know me may think I have no business writing such a book as *Lead Serve Love*. Indeed, I am a depraved, morally bankrupt, wretched sinner through and through. I've attended church sporadically most of my life, haven't spent a minute in seminary, and only recently gave the Bible more than a cursory review. I've attended exactly one theology class, and I dropped out of it.

However, despite my moral infidelity, I've come to be filled with the Holy Spirit. I've learned my salvation isn't the result of what I do but rather what Jesus has done on my behalf. It is only fitting I give my first thanks in this acknowledgment to my Lord, my God, my Father, who through his grace gave me the words contained herein in the first place. Praise the Lord, for even an unworthy, chronic sinner such as I can experience his glory!

I would also like to thank all the people God put in my path to help me bring this book from an idea to a reality: Kristina Holmes, my agent who embraced this book right away and worked tirelessly to steward it to publication; Laura Minchew, MacKenzie Howard, Lisa Stilwell, and Michelle Burke of Thomas Nelson; Scott "Chip" Traynor, who shared with me the simplicity and wisdom of a "three-ology theology"; Randy Pope, Steve Brown, Matt Ballard, and David McNeely, who inspire me from the pulpit; Debra Potter, Jackie Dieter, Chip Sweney, and Drue Warner, the salt and light in my days as we work together for kingdom impact; Keith Compton and the other guys of the Men's Discipleship Group, who hold me accountable; Ginny Baker, my friend who encouraged me immensely along the first steps of my walk; and countless others in my Perimeter Church family who have shown me abundant love and grace.

Finally, and mentioned last only so I can set her apart, I thank my dear wife, Jill. She is indeed the answer to many prayers, the sweetest taste of life I have in this world, and the most attractive editor and critic I've ever had the pleasure of working with. Thank you, my dear, for inspiring me, encouraging me, loving me, indulging me, admonishing me, and forgiving me. You leave me with no doubt there are indeed angels among us this present day.

To contact the author: gregoryelang@gmail.com

May the Lord bless us and keep us, and may his love shine through in everything we do.

AMEN.